D0530082

SCiENCE to 14

Stephen Pople

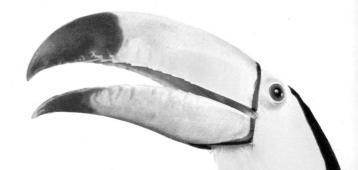

Oxford University Press

Oxford University Press, Walton Street, Oxford OX2 6DP

Oxford   New York
Athens   Auckland   Bangkok   Bombay
Calcutta   Cape Town   Dar es Salaam   Delhi
Florence   Hong Kong   Istanbul   Karachi
Kuala Lumpur   Madras   Madrid   Melbourne
Mexico City   Nairobi   Paris   Singapore
Tapei   Tokyo   Toronto

and associated companies in
Berlin   Ibadan

Oxford is a trademark of the Oxford University Press

Typeset in Univers 45 Light

Printed in Spain by Gráficas Estella

ISBN 0 19 914582 2 (net edition)
       0 19 914577 6 (non net edition)

Acknowledgements

*The publisher would like to thank the following agencies for their kind
permission to reproduce the following photographs:*

AEA Technology p 60; Allsport pp 98, 102; Ancient Art & Architecture p 66;
Bruce Coleman Photo Library /D Spears p 10, /T Bucholz p 13, /J Shaw p 14;
Colorsport pp 90, 101; GeoScience Features p 46 (all); J Allan Cash pp 48, 68,
69, 72, 75, 94, 114; Oxford Scientific Films /A Walsh p 35, /S Rowner p 37,
/B Kent p 43, /U Walz 92; Science Photo Library pp 26 (all), 27, 78, 109,
/Dr K Schiller p 19, /CNRI p 20, 29, /D Scharf p 24, /Dr G Settles p 28,
/Dr J Burgess p 31, /R Ressmeyer p 56, /H Schneebeli p 82, /A Bartel p 89,
/D Parker p 111, /M Dohrn p 116, /NASA p 119; Spectrum Colour Library pp 72,
107; Zefa Photographic Library pp 38 (all), 62, 64.

Additional photography by Chris Honeywell.

The illustrations are by:

Chris Duggan, Jones Sewell, Pat Murray, Mike Ogden, Pat Thorne,
Borin Van Loon, and Pamela Venus.

Contents

Introduction

If you are working towards Key Stage 3 (levels 3 to 7) of the Science National Curriculum, then this book is designed for you. It explains the science concepts that you will meet, and helps you find what you need to know. The topics are covered in double-page units which we have called **spreads**.

Contents Here, you can see how the spreads are arranged.

Test and check Try answering these questions when you revise. At the end of each question, there is a number telling you which spread to look up if you need to check information or find out more.

Spread 1.1 This tells you how to plan and carry out an investigation and interpret the results.

Spreads 2.2 to 4.21 These are grouped into three sections, matching Attainment Targets 2, 3, and 4 of the National Curriculum. Within each section, the spreads have been arranged in the same order as the strands of the National Curriculum.

Summaries These tell you the main points covered in sections 2, 3, and 4, and the particular spreads which deal with them.

Answers to questions Here, you will find brief answers to *all* the questions in the spreads, not just the numerical ones. But try the questions before you look at the answers!

Index Use this if you have a particular scientific word or term which you need to look up.

To be a good scientist, you need to carry out investigations. This book should help you to understand the scientific ideas which support your investigations. I hope that you will find it useful.

Stephen Pople

Test and check

Can you answer the following? The spread number in brackets tells you where to find the information.

1 What eight features do animals and plants have in common? *(2.1)*

2 Which part of a cell is the 'control centre'? *(2.1)*

3 How do plant cells and animal cells differ? *(2.1)*

4 How do plants obtain their food? What is the process called? *(2.2)*

5 How do plants and animals get their energy? What is the process called? *(2.2)*

6 Where in a flower are the male sex cells and the female sex cells? *(2.3)*

7 How can pollen be transferred from one flower to another? *(2.3)*

8 In a flower, what happens after fertilization? *(2.3)*

9 What are the three main jobs done by your skeleton? *(2.4)*

10 Why do muscles work in pairs? *(2.4)*

11 What is the central nervous system? What does it do? *(2.4)*

12 What happens to food in the gut? *(2.5)*

13 What are the five main types of nutrient in food? *(2.5)*

14 Can you describe five important jobs done by the blood? *(2.6)*

15 What is the difference between arteries and veins? *(2.6)*

16 Why does the heart need to work as two separate pumps? *(2.6)*

17 What job is done by the lungs? *(2.7)*

18 Can you describe some of the jobs done by the liver? *(2.7)*

19 What do the kidneys do? *(2.7)*

20 How often do a woman's ovaries release an ovum? *(2.8)*

21 How is an ovum fertilized? What happens to it if it is fertilized? *(2.8)*

22 What happens if the ovum is not fertilized? *(2.8)*

23 In the uterus, how does a developing baby get its food and oxygen? *(2.9)*

24 Why should a woman avoid smoking when she is pregnant? *(2.9)*

25 What are germs? How can they spread from one person to another? *(2.10)*

26 How does your body defend itself against germs? *(2.10)*

27 How can you help your body defend itself against germs? *(2.10)*

28 Can you describe four methods of preserving food and explain why they work? *(2.11)*

29 Can you give three examples of ways in which microbes are useful? *(2.11)*

30 What happens during fermentation? *(2.11)*

31 Can you use a key to identify a plant or animal? *(2.12)*

32 What feature do vertebrates have in common? *(2.12)*

33 What are the five main groups of vertebrates? *(2.12)*

34 Can you give two examples of inherited characteristics? *(2.13)*

35 Where is information about your inherited characteristics stored? *(2.13)*

36 Can you give an example of how the environment can affect a characteristic? *(2.13)*

37 Can you give an example of selective breeding? *(2.13)*

38 Can you name one living and one non-living factor that can affect a population of animals or plants? *(2.14)*

39 Can you give an example of how an animal or plant is adapted to its environment? *(2.14)*

40 Humans grow crops. How can this affect other populations of plants and animals? *(2.15)*

41 Can you describe five different types of pollution caused by humans? *(2.15)*

42 Can you give an example of a food chain? *(2.16)*

43 Why are most food chains only three or four organisms long? *(2.16)*

44 What are decomposers? What do they do? *(2.16)*

45 How can carbon atoms in the atmosphere end up in the body of an animal? How are they returned to the atmosphere? *(2.17)*

46 How can nitrogen atoms in the atmosphere end up in the body of an animal? How are they returned to the atmosphere? *(2.17)*

Test and check

Can you answer the following? The spread number in brackets tells you where to find the information.

1   What differences are there between a solid, a liquid, and a gas? *(3.1)*

2   What are the main properties of metals, ceramics, plastics, glasses, and fibres? *(3.1)*

3   What is the difference between an element and a compound? *(3.2)*

4   What does the reactivity series tell you about different metals? *(3.2)*

5   What is the difference between a mixture and a compound? *(3.3)*

6   What is a solute? What is a solvent? What is a solution? *(3.3)*

7   How would you separate sand from salt? *(3.3)*

8   How would you separate copper(II) sulphate from water? *(3.3)*

9   How would you separate salt from water? *(3.3)*

10 How would you separate the different inks in a mixture? *(3.3)*

11 What gas is given off when an acid reacts with a metal? *(3.4)*

12 How does an acid affect litmus indicator? *(3.4)*

13 How does an alkali affect litmus indicator? *(3.4)*

14 If a solution has a pH of 1, what does tell you about it? *(3.4)*

15 If a solution has a pH of 7, what does tell you about it? *(3.4)*

16 If a base neutralizes an acid what is produced? *(3.4)*

17 In the periodic table, in what ways are elements in the same group similar? *(3.5)*

18 What is meant by a change of state? *(3.6)*

19 When ice melts, what happens to its particles? *(3.6)*

20 When water evaporates, what happens to its particles? *(3.6)*

21 Why does a steel bar expand when heated? *(3.6)*

22 What is absolute zero on the Celsius scale? *(3.7)*

23 What is absolute zero on the Kelvin scale? *(3.7)*

24 What is the link between the pressure, volume, and temperature of a fixed mass of gas? *(3.7)*

25 What three types of particle make up an atom? *(3.8)*

26 What is an ion? *(3.8)*

27 What is the difference between ionic bonding and covalent bonding? *(3.8)*

28 What is a molecule? *(3.8)*

29 What are the three main types of nuclear radiation? How are they different? *(3.9)*

30 What is the difference between an exothermic chemical reaction and an endothermic one? *(3.10)*

31 How can you tell whether a chemical reaction has taken place? *(3.10)*

32 What factors affect the rate of a chemical reaction? *(3.10)*

33 If an element burns in oxygen, what is the product? *(3.11)*

34 If a fuel such as methane burns, what are the products? *(3.11)*

35 What is the combustion triangle? *(3.11)*

36 Can you give an example of food oxidation? *(3.11)*

37 If a metal has become corroded, what has happened on its surface? *(3.11)*

38 Why is gold found in the ground as a pure metal, while iron is only found in compounds? *(3.12)*

39 How is iron produced from iron ore? *(3.12)*

40 What is steel? How is it made? *(3.12)*

41 Why are some metals more difficult to separate from their ores than others? *(3.12)*

42 What metals are produced by electrolysis? *(3.12)*

43 How many uses or products of common salt can you think of? *(3.13)*

44 What is limestone used for? *(3.13)*

45 What are the main fractions in oil? What are they used for? *(3.14)*

46 What are the two main gases in air? What are they used for? *(3.14)*

47 How are clouds formed? *(3.15)*

48 What causes winds? *(3.15)*

49 What are depressions? What weather do they bring, and why? *(3.15)*

50 What is the water cycle? *(3.16)*

51 What is the rock cycle? *(3.16)*

52 What are the three main types of rock in the Earth's crust? How are they each formed? *(3.17)*

Test and check

Can you answer the following? The spread number in brackets tells you where to find the information.

1 Which materials are the best conductors of electricity? *(4.1)*

2 What happens when like charges are brought close? *(4.1)*

3 How does a switch stop a current flowing? *(4.1)*

4 Can you draw a simple circuit with a battery and two bulbs a) in series b) in parallel? What are the advantages of the parallel arrangement? *(4.2)*

5 Why do heating elements get hot, while copper connecting wires do not? *(4.3)*

6 What does 'kW h' stand for? What does it measure? *(4.3)*

7 Can you describe some uses of logic gates? *(4.4)*

8 Can you write truth tables for AND, OR, and NOT gates and explain what they mean? *(4.4)*

9 What happens when like poles of two magnets are brought close? *(4.5)*

10 Why would the core of an electromagnet be made of iron rather than steel? *(4.5)*

11 How many uses of electromagnets can you describe? *(4.5)*

12 What produces the turning effect in an electric motor? *(4.6)*

13 What is an alternator? How does it work? *(4.6)*

14 What do AC and DC stand for? What is the difference between them? *(4.6)*

15 What are transformers used for? *(4.6)*

16 How many different types of energy can you list? Can you give an example of each type? *(4.7)*

17 What is the law of conservation of energy? *(4.7)*

18 In what ways can heat travel? *(4.8)*

19 Why are wool and fur good insulators? *(4.8)*

20 If a power station has an efficiency of 35%, what does this mean? *(4.9)*

21 Can you explain the difference between a non-renewable and a renewable energy source? Can you give an example of each type? *(4.9)*

22 Can you explain how the energy in petrol originally came from the Sun? *(4.10)*

23 What unit is used to measure force? *(4.11)*

24 What are the forces on a parachutist descending at steady speed? How do they compare? *(4.11)*

25 How do you calculate pressure? *(4.11)*

26 How do you calculate the moment of a force? *(4.12)*

27 What is the law of moments? *(4.12)*

28 What features make one thing less likely to topple over than another? *(4.12)*

29 How do you calculate average speed? *(4.13)*

30 Can you give two ways in which friction is useful and two ways in which it is a nuisance? *(4.13)*

31 When a car has to slow down, what is meant by the 'thinking distance'? *(4.13)*

32 Can you name a machine which is a) a force magnifier b) a movement magnifier? *(4.14)*

33 How do you calculate work done? *(4.14)*

34 How do you calculate power? *(4.14)*

35 What causes sound waves? *(4.15)*

36 Why cannot sound travel through a vacuum? *(4.15)*

37 How could an echo be used to calculate the speed of sound? *(4.15)*

38 What happens inside your ear when sound waves are received? *(4.16)*

39 Comparing sound waves, how are loud sounds different from quiet sounds? How are high sounds different from low sounds? *(4.16)*

40 How does a flat mirror form an image? *(4.17)*

41 Why do light rays bend when they enter glass? What is the effect called? *(4.17)*

42 How do optical fibres work? *(4.17)*

43 How is the image formed in a camera? In what ways is the eye similar to a camera? *(4.18)*

44 What happens to white light when it passes through a prism? *(4.19)*

45 Can you list the different types of waves in the electromagnetic spectrum? *(4.19)*

46 What keeps the Earth in orbit around the Sun? *(4.20)*

47 Why do we get seasons? *(4.20)*

48 Why do we see different phases of the Moon? *(4.20)*

49 What is a galaxy? Why are humans never likely to visit other galaxies? *(4.21)*

1·1 How to investigate

This spread should help you to
- *plan a scientific investigation*
- *carry out your investigation*
- *interpret your results*

The left-hand side of each page describes in stages what to do. The right-hand side shows one student's thoughts about one particular investigation.

Planning

- **Decide on a problem to investigate**

  In the example shown on the right, the student has decided to investigate how quickly sugar dissolves in water.

- **Write down your hypothesis**

  You may already have an idea of what you expect to happen in your investigation. This idea is called your **hypothesis**. It may not be right! It is just an idea, though it may be based on work in science which you have done before. The aim of your investigation is to test your idea.

- **Decide what variables you are dealing with**

  Things like temperature, particle size, mass, and colour are all called **variables**. They are things you can measure or observe, but they can *change* from one situation to another.

  In your investigation, you have to decide what the variables are, which ones you will keep fixed, and which you will change.

  To make sense of your results, you need to change just one variable at a time, and find out how it affects one other. If lots of variables change at once, it won't be a fair test. For example, if you want to find out how particle size affects dissolving, it wouldn't be fair to compare big, brown sugar crystals in hot water with small, white ones in cold water.

- **Decide what equipment you need, and in what order you will do things**

  Before you do this read **Carrying out** on the next page first.

- **Prepare tables for your results**

  Before you do this read **Carrying out** on the next page first.

I will investigate how quickly sugar dissolves in water.

Sugar is made up of molecules. These stick together to make bigger particles (sugar crystals). In icing sugar, the particles are very tiny. In caster sugar, they are a bit bigger. In ordinary sugar, they are a bit bigger again.

If the particles are small, the water can get in contact with all the sugar more quickly. So I think that small particles will dissolve more quickly than big ones.

I also think that sugar particles will dissolve more quickly in hot water. The water molecules will be moving faster, so they will bump into sugar molecules more often.

The main variables I will be dealing with are:
   time for the sugar to dissolve
   particle size
   temperature

Other variables are the amount of sugar, amount of water, the type of sugar (brown or white), and whether I stir it or not. I will use the same amounts of sugar and water each time. I will use white sugar. And I will stir gently, because that separates the particles. If the particles are in a heap, the water cannot reach them properly.

Items needed:
   ordinary sugar, caster sugar, icing sugar
   beaker
   thermometer

Carrying out

- **Choose the instruments you need**
  You may need to measure with instruments like thermometers and stopwatches. But for some observations, you may just be using your eyes!

- **Carry out your investigation, and record your measurements and observations**
  You will need a table for each set of readings.

Interpreting results

- **Look for patterns in your results**
  One way of doing this is to plot a graph, showing how one variable changes with another.

- **Compare your conclusions with your original idea**
  Do your results support your original hypothesis?

- **Present your conclusions**
  What links did you find between any of the variables?
  How would you explain these links? Does your original hypothesis help?

- **Assess your investigation**
  How sure are you of your findings? How accurate do you think your results are? How do you think your investigation could be improved?

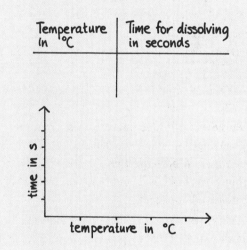

First, I will find out how temperature affects dissolving. I will use ordinary sugar each time, so that particle size is fixed. I will dissolve the sugar in water at different temperatures. When I do this, I will measure the temperature with a thermometer, and the time for dissolving with a stopwatch.

Next, I will see how particle size affects dissolving. I might be able to measure the size of the sugar crystals with a microscope. If not, I will just call them 'small', 'medium', and 'large'.

Temperature in °C	Time for dissolving in seconds

time in s

temperature in °C

There seems to be a link between time for dissolving and temperature. As the temperature gets higher, the time for dissolving gets....

This is why I think there is a link. When the temperature rises, the water molecules move faster, and.....

Measuring the time accurately was difficult. It was hard to tell when all the sugar had dissolved. Also, I would like to measure the particle size more accurately.

Looking at life

By the end of this spread, you should be able to:
- *describe the features which are common to living things*
- *describe the differences between animal cells and plant cells*

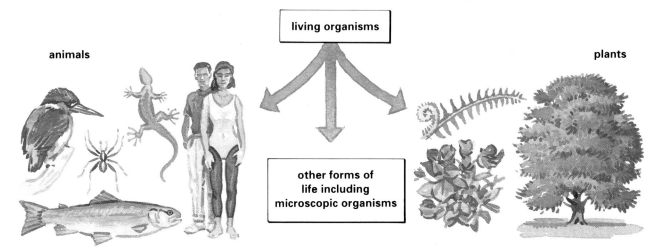

animals

living organisms

plants

other forms of
life including
microscopic organisms

Features of life

Animals and plants are ***living organisms***. They have these features in common:

Feeding Animals and plants need food. Animals must take in food. Plants take in simple materials like water and carbon dioxide gas. They use these, and the energy in sunlight, to make their own food.

Respiration (releasing energy from food) Animals and plants need energy to stay alive, grow, and move. Usually, they get their energy from chemical reactions between food and oxygen.

Excretion (getting rid of waste products) Animals and plants produce waste materials which they must get rid of. For example, you excrete when you breathe out 'used' air, or go to the toilet.

Growth Animals and plants grow bigger. They may also grow new parts to replace old or damaged ones.

Movement Animals and plants can move, though animals usually make bigger and faster movements than plants.

Reproduction Animals and plants can produce more of their own kind. For example, humans have children.

Sensitivity Animals and plants react to the outside world. For example, they may be sensitive to light or a change in temperature. Animals usually react much more quickly than plants.

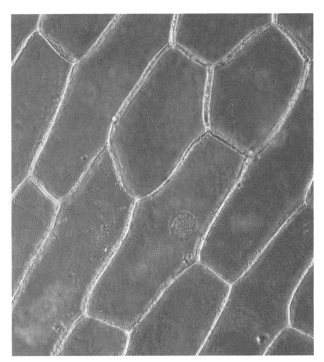

Onion cells: magnification x700

Cells Animals and plants are made from tiny, living units called cells. Respiration takes place in cells. So do all the other chemical reactions needed for life. Living organisms grow by ***cell division***. A cell grows and splits to form two new cells. Then these cells grow and split.... and so on.

Animal cells

Animal cells exist in many shapes and sizes. But they all have several features in common:

Nucleus This controls all the chemical reactions that take place in the cell. It contains, thread-like **chromosomes** which store the chemical instructions needed to build the cell.

Cell membrane This is a thin skin which controls the movement of materials in and out of the cell.

Cytoplasm In this jelly, the cell's vital chemical reactions take place. New substances are made, and energy is released and stored. Sometimes, cytoplasm contains tiny droplets of liquid called **vacuoles**.

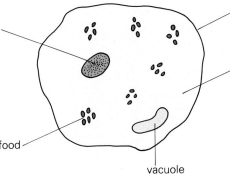

stored food

vacuole

Plant cells

Plant cells also have a **cell membrane**, **cytoplasm**, and **nucleus**. But they have certain features which make them different from animal cells:

Cell wall Plant cells are surrounded by a firm wall made of **cellulose**. This holds plant cells together and gives them much of their strength. For example, wood is mainly cellulose.

Chloroplasts These contain a green substance called **chlorophyll**. This absorbs the energy in sunlight. Plants need the energy to make their food.

Cell sap This is a watery liquid in a large vacuole. Pressure from the liquid keep the cell firm, rather like a tiny balloon. If a plant loses too much liquid from its cells, the pressure falls and the plant wilts.

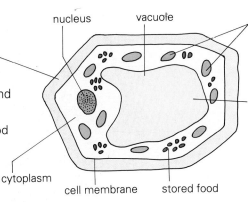

nucleus   vacuole

cytoplasm

cell membrane   stored food

Groups of cells

Complicated organisms like you and me are made of billions of cells. Different groups of cells have different jobs to do. Groups of similar cells are called **tissue**. A collection of tissues doing a particular job is called an **organ**. Eyes are organs, so are muscles.

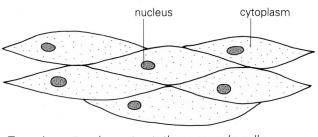

nucleus   cytoplasm

To make a muscle contract, these muscle cells shorten

1 In what ways are living things different from non-living things?
2 In what ways are animals different from plants?
3 Animals and plants show *sensitivity*. Give an example to explain what this means.
4 Give *three* ways in which plant cells are similar to animal cells.
5 Give *three* ways in which plant cells are different from animal cells.
6 What are *chloroplasts* and what do they contain?
7 What job is done by the *nucleus* of a cell?
8 What is meant by *respiration*? Where in the body of an animal or plant does it take place?
9 What is *tissue*? What is the name for a collection of tissues doing one particular job?

Making and using food

By the end of this spread, you should be able to:
- *explain how plants make their food*
- *explain why animals and plants respire*
- *name the gases involved in making and using food*

Living things need food. It supplies them with materials for growth, and energy for maintaining life. Animals have to find their food. But plants make their own.

Photosynthesis

Plants take in carbon dioxide gas from the air, and water from the soil. They use the energy in sunlight to turn these into food such as glucose sugar. The process is called **photosynthesis**.

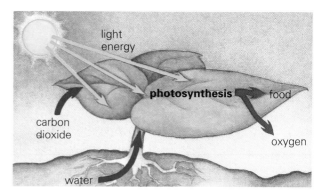

This equation summarizes what happens during photosynthesis:

$$\text{carbon dioxide} + \text{water} \xrightarrow{\text{light energy}} \text{sugar} + \text{oxygen}$$

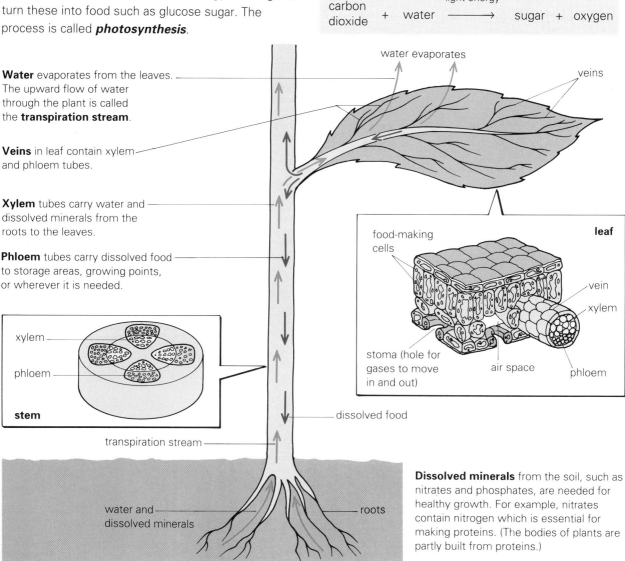

Water evaporates from the leaves. The upward flow of water through the plant is called the **transpiration stream**.

Veins in leaf contain xylem and phloem tubes.

Xylem tubes carry water and dissolved minerals from the roots to the leaves.

Phloem tubes carry dissolved food to storage areas, growing points, or wherever it is needed.

water evaporates

veins

food-making cells

leaf

vein

xylem

stoma (hole for gases to move in and out)

air space

phloem

xylem

phloem

stem

transpiration stream

dissolved food

water and dissolved minerals

roots

Dissolved minerals from the soil, such as nitrates and phosphates, are needed for healthy growth. For example, nitrates contain nitrogen which is essential for making proteins. (The bodies of plants are partly built from proteins.)

To absorb the energy in sunlight, plants have a green chemical called chlorophyll in their leaves.

During photosynthesis, plants make oxygen as well as food. They need some of this oxygen. But the rest comes out of their leaves through tiny holes called **stomata** (each hole is called a **stoma**). The same holes are also used for taking in carbon dioxide.

When plants make their food, they can store it in their leaves and roots to be used later on. Some is stored in the form of **starch**. By eating plants, animals can use this stored food.

Respiration

Plants and animals get energy from their food by a chemical process called **respiration**. It is rather like burning, but without any flames. Usually, the food is combined with oxygen:

food + oxygen → carbon dioxide + water + *energy*

Carbon dioxide and water are the waste products. For example, the air you breathe out contains extra carbon dioxide and water vapour produced by respiration.

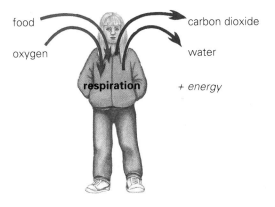

Gases in balance

Respiration takes place all the time. So plants and animals need a steady supply of oxygen.

During daylight hours, plants make oxygen by photosynthesis. They make more than they need for respiration, so they put their spare oxygen into the atmosphere.

At night, photosynthesis stops. So plants must take in oxygen - just like animals. However, they use less oxygen during the night than they give out during the day.

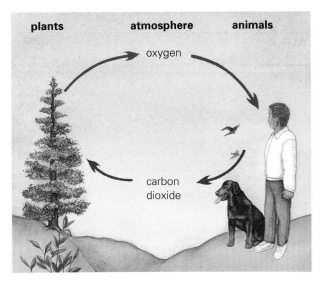

Overall, plants take in carbon dioxide and give out oxygen, while animals take in oxygen and give out carbon dioxide. Between them, they keep the gases in the atmosphere in balance.

1 During photosynthesis, what gas is
   a) used up b) made?
2 What else do plants make during photosynthesis?
3 Why does photosynthesis usually stop at night?
4 Why do plants need minerals from the soil?
5 Where do gases enter and leave a plant?
6 What is a *transpiration stream*?
7 During respiration, what gas is usually
   a) used up
   b) made?
8 Animals are using up oxygen all the time. Why does the amount of oxygen in the atmosphere not go down?

Reproducing with flowers

By the end of this spread, you should be able to:
* explain what the different parts of a flower do
* describe how seeds are formed and scattered
* describe how seeds grow

Some plants produce flowers. They have flowers so that they can reproduce themselves. Flowers contain the tiny male and female cells which, when combined, grow into seeds.

Flowers

Parts of a flower

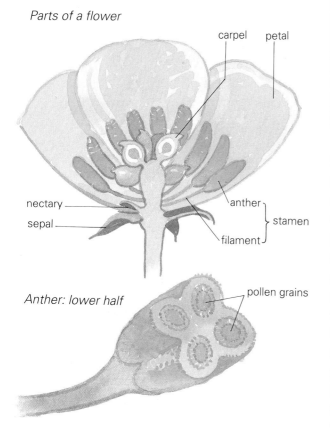

Anther: lower half

Some flowers contain **male sex cells**. Some contain **female sex cells**. But many contain both types.

Stamens hold the grains of **pollen** which contain the male sex cells. Pollen in released when the **anther** ripens and splits open.

Carpels have a space inside called an **ovary**. In the ovary are tiny **ovules**, each containing a female sex cell. When the tip of a carpel is ripe, it is ready to receive grains of pollen.

Pollination

Before a male sex cell can combine with a female sex cell, pollen grains must be transferred to the tip of a carpel. This process is called **pollination**.

Self-pollination means that pollen is transferred from stamens to carpels on the *same plant*.

Cross-pollination means that pollen is transferred from stamens to carpels on *another plant* of the same type. There are different ways in which this can happen:

Insect-pollinated plants Insects, such as bees, carry pollen on their bodies as they move from flower to flower. The insects are attracted to the flowers by their scent or bright colours. They search for the sugary nectar inside.

Wind-pollinated plants Pollen is carried by the wind from one plant to another. The flowers are not usually brightly coloured, but they have parts which hang out in the wind.

Cross-pollination gives a wider variety of young plants than self-pollination. This helps in the struggle for survival. To prevent self-pollination, flowers often have stamens and carpels which ripen at different times.

Fertilization

When a pollen grain sticks to a ripe carpel, a pollen tube may grow out of the grain and down to an ovule. A nucleus from a male sex cell can pass down this tube and combine with the nucleus of the female sex cell. If this happens, the cell has been **fertilized**.

Seeds and fruits

A complete ovary after fertilization is called a **fruit**. In the ovary, each fertilized cell grows by cell division to form a **seed**. This has a thick coat for protection.

Plants try to scatter their seeds over a large area so that some may survive to grow into new plants. The scattering of seeds is called **dispersal**. Different plants use different methods. Here are some of them:

- Seeds have hooks so that they can be carried by animals.
- Fruits are eaten by animals. The seeds come out with the droppings.
- Seeds are shaped so that they can be carried by the wind.
- Seeds are in pods. These pop open when dry and flick out the seeds.

Germination

If a seed absorbs water, and the temperature and air conditions are right, it may begin to grow. Scientists say that the seed **germinates**.

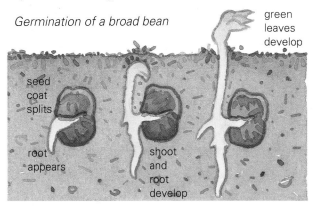

Germination of a broad bean

green leaves develop

seed coat splits

root appears

shoot and root develop

When a seed germinates, a tiny shoot grows upwards, and a root grows downwards. The root and shoot are sensitive to the direction of gravity. The shoot may also be sensitive to light. For example, when it comes out of the soil, it may bend towards the light. Growth in a particular direction, because of light, gravity, or other influence is called a **tropism**.

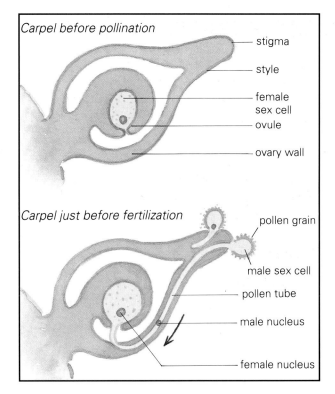

Carpel before pollination

- stigma
- style
- female sex cell
- ovule
- ovary wall

Carpel just before fertilization

- pollen grain
- male sex cell
- pollen tube
- male nucleus
- female nucleus

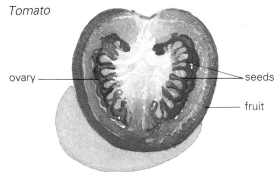

Tomato

- ovary
- seeds
- fruit

1 Which part of a flower contains a) the female sex cells b) the male sex cells?
2 What is the difference between *self-pollination* and *cross-pollination*?
3 Describe *two* ways in which cross-pollination can take place.
4 Why are some flowers brightly coloured?
5 Once pollen grains have stuck to a carpel, how does fertilization take place?
6 In a flower, what do the ovaries become after fertilization?
7 In what ways do plants disperse their seeds?
8 What is meant by *germination*?
9 Why do seeds need a thick coat?
10 Give an example of a *tropism*.

The body in action

By the end of this spread, you should be able to:
- *describe the jobs done by the skeleton*
- *describe how muscles move the body*
- *explain how the body is controlled*

The skeleton

Your body is supported by a framework of rigid bones called a *skeleton*. This has several important jobs to do:

Support The skeleton allows you to stand upright on the ground. It also supports vital organs inside your body.

Protection The skeleton protects many organs:

The *skull* protects the brain. The *ribs* form a cage which protects the heart and lungs. The *vertebral column* (backbone) protects the spinal cord.

Movement Many parts of the skeleton are jointed so that you can move bits of your body. The movements are made by muscles fixed to the skeleton.

Some joints just allow small movements. For example, your back can bend a little because the vertebrae have *cartilage* (gristle) discs sandwiched between them. The discs also absorb jolts.

Bone contains living cells, surrounded by hard minerals for strength. Calcium is the main mineral used. Bone is also reinforced by tough **collagen** fibres which give it even more strength.

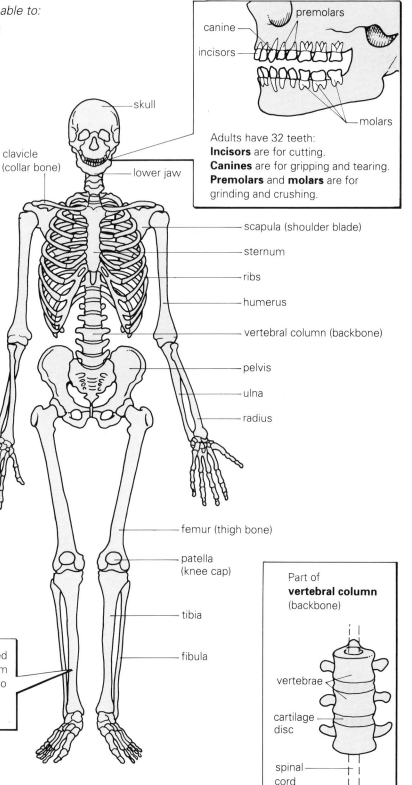

Adults have 32 teeth:
Incisors are for cutting.
Canines are for gripping and tearing.
Premolars and **molars** are for grinding and crushing.

canine
premolars
incisors
molars

skull
clavicle (collar bone)
lower jaw
scapula (shoulder blade)
sternum
ribs
humerus
vertebral column (backbone)
pelvis
ulna
radius
femur (thigh bone)
patella (knee cap)
tibia
fibula

Part of
vertebral column
(backbone)

vertebrae
cartilage disc
spinal cord

Joints and muscles

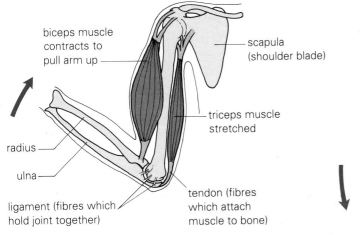

biceps muscle contracts to pull arm up

scapula (shoulder blade)

triceps muscle stretched

radius

ulna

ligament (fibres which hold joint together)

tendon (fibres which attach muscle to bone)

Raising arm

antagonistic pair of muscles

biceps muscle stretched

triceps muscle contracts to pull arm down

synovial fluid lubricates joint

Lowering arm

Many joints are like hinges or swivels. The joints in your arms are like this. Muscles move joints by contracting (getting shorter). However, a muscle cannot lengthen itself. It has to be pulled back to its original shape. That is why muscles are often arranged in **antagonistic pairs**. One muscle pulls the joint one way, the other pulls it back.

Sense and control

Your body is controlled by the **central nervous system** (the brain and spinal cord). This is linked to all parts of the body by **nerves**. Signals called **nerve impulses** travel along these nerves. The central nervous system use them to sense what is happening inside and outside the body and to control the actions of muscles and organs. For example, if you see a wasp on your hand, your eyes send signals to your brain. This sends signals to muscles, making them contract so that your hand moves.

Signals sent to the central nervous system come from **sensor cells**. The table below shows some of the things these cells respond to:

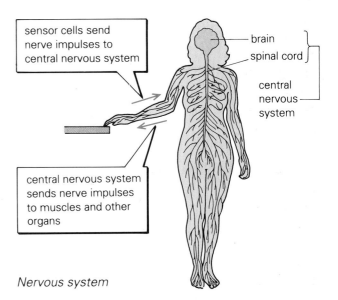

sensor cells send nerve impulses to central nervous system

brain

spinal cord

central nervous system

central nervous system sends nerve impulses to muscles and other organs

Nervous system

Sensors cells in...	respond to
eyes	light
ears	sound
nose	chemicals in air
tongue	chemicals in food
skin	touch, pressure, heat, pain

1 Which parts of the human body are protected by a) the skull b) the ribs c) the vertebral column?
2 The vertebrae have cartilage discs sandwiched between them. What do these discs do?
3 Apart from protection, what other jobs are done by the skeleton?
4 What is the main mineral in bone? What else gives bone its strength?
5 What are a) tendons b) ligaments?
6 Why do muscles work in pairs?
7 You hear a loud noise and it makes you jump. Use your ideas about the nervous system to explain how a loud noise makes you jump.

Dealing with food

By the end of this spread, you should be able to:
- *describe what happens to food in the body*
- *describe the foods needed for a balanced diet*

When you eat food, much of it ends up, dissolved, in your blood. This carries food to all the cells of your body. The cells use it for energy, and for making the materials needed for living and growing.

The gut

When you swallow food, it moves down a long tube called the **alimentary canal** or **gut**. This runs from the mouth to the anus. Two important things happen to food as it passes along the gut:

Food is digested This means that it is broken down into simpler substances which will dissolve. The chemicals which do this are called **enzymes**. Enzymes are **catalysts**: they speed up chemical reactions without being used up themselves.

Digestion mainly takes place in the stomach and small intestine. But it begins in the mouth. As you chew, an enzyme called **amylase** in your saliva starts to break down any starch into a type of sugar called **glucose**.

Digested food is absorbed into the blood Once food has dissolved, it can pass into the blood. This mainly happens in the small intestine. Its walls are lined with tiny blood tubes which carry the digested food away.

Undigested matter passes into the large intestine. Here most of its water is reabsorbed by the body. This leaves a semi-solid waste (faeces) which comes out of the anus when you go to the toilet.

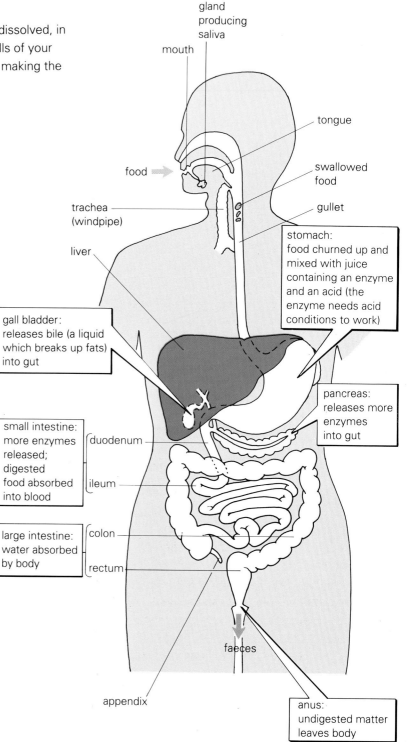

gland producing saliva

mouth

tongue

food ➡

swallowed food

trachea (windpipe)

gullet

liver

stomach:
food churned up and mixed with juice containing an enzyme and an acid (the enzyme needs acid conditions to work)

gall bladder:
releases bile (a liquid which breaks up fats) into gut

pancreas:
releases more enzymes into gut

small intestine:
more enzymes released; digested food absorbed into blood

duodenum

ileum

large intestine:
water absorbed by body

colon

rectum

faeces

appendix

anus:
undigested matter leaves body

Nutrients

The useful substances in our food are called **nutrients**. The five main types of nutrient are shown in the table below.

A balanced diet is one which supplies the right amounts of *all* the nutrients. A poor diet can lead to health problems (see Spread 2.10).

Nutrients	Examples		
Carbohydrates Supply about 50% of our energy	*Sugars* Jam, cakes, sweets, glucose, sweet fruits *The body breaks down sugars and starches into simple sugars like glucose. Some may be converted into fats.*	*Starches* Potatoes, rice, bread, flour	*Cellulose* Vegetables, cereal foods *Cellulose cannot be used by the body as a nutrient, but it provides bulk (dietary fibre or 'roughage') to help food pass through the system more easily.*
Fats Supply about 40% of our energy	Butter, margarine, lard, meat *Fats can be stored by the body; they provide a reserve supply of food.*		
Proteins Supply materials for growth	Meat, eggs, fish, milk, cheese, bread *The body breaks down proteins into amino acids which it can use to build new body tissues*		
Minerals Needed for some body tissues and some chemical reactions	Minerals needed by the body include: Calcium *(for teeth and bones)* – from cheese, milk, vegetables Iron *(used in making blood)* – from liver, eggs, bread Sodium *(for muscle movements)* – from salt		
Vitamins Needed to speed up some chemical reactions	Vitamins needed by the body include: **Vitamin A** – from green vegetables, carrots, liver, butter. *a shortage of vitamin A weakens your vision in the dark* **Vitamin B$_1$** (thiamine) – from yeast, bread, meat, potatoes, milk. **Vitamin B$_2$** (riboflavine) – from fresh milk, liver, eggs. **Vitamin C** – from blackcurrants, green vegetables, oranges. *a shortage of vitamin C causes a disease called scurvy* **Vitamin D** – cod liver oil, margarine, eggs. *a shortage of vitamin D causes rickets (soft bones)* *Your skin makes vitamin D when exposed to sunlight*		

1 Food is *digested*. What does this mean?
2 Where does digestion mainly take place?
3 What are *enzymes*?
4 What happens to food in the stomach?
5 What happens to food after it has been digested?
6 What happens to undigested food?
7 What are the five main types of nutrient?
8 Which nutrients supply us with most of our energy?
9 Why does the body need a) proteins b) calcium? Name some foods which can suppy a) and b).
10 Why does the body need vitamins?
11 The body cannot digest fibre (cellulose). Why is it still important in our diet?

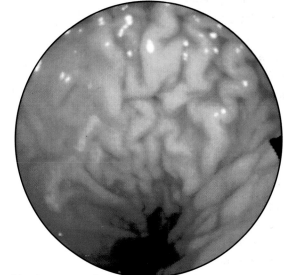

Inside the stomach

The blood system

By the end of this spread, you should be able to:
* explain what blood is and what it does
* describe how blood is pumped round the body

Blood

Blood is a mixture of **red cells**, **white cells**, and **platelets**, in a watery liquid called **plasma**.

There are hundreds of times more red cells than white. It is the red cells which give blood its red colour.

Jobs done by the blood

* Bringing oxygen, water, and digested food (such as glucose) to the cells of the body.
* Taking carbon dioxide and other waste products away from the cells.
* Distributing heat to all parts of the body.
* Carrying **hormones** round the body. (Hormones are chemicals which control how different organs work.)
* Carrying substances which help fight disease.

Red cells These are partly made from a protein called **haemoglobin**. This can pick up oxygen. When red cells are carrying oxygen, their colour is a brighter red.

Plasma This is mainly water, with digested food, hormones, antibodies, and carbon dioxide dissolved in it.

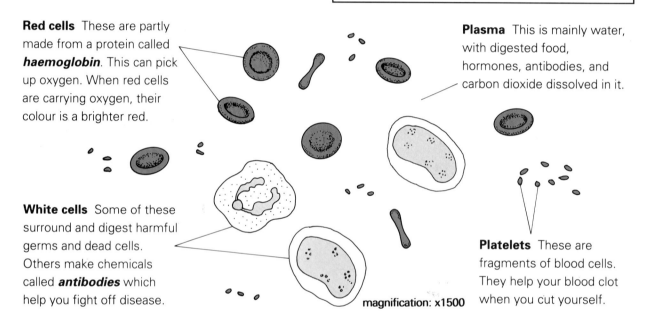

White cells Some of these surround and digest harmful germs and dead cells. Others make chemicals called **antibodies** which help you fight off disease.

magnification: x1500

Platelets These are fragments of blood cells. They help your blood clot when you cut yourself.

False colour photo of red blood cells in a capillary: magnification x1800

Circulating blood

The heart pumps blood round the body through a system of tubes.

Arteries Blood leaves the heart at high pressure through wide tubes called arteries.

Capillaries The arteries divide into narrower tubes. These carry the blood to networks of very fine tubes called capillaries. Every living cell in the body is close to a capillary. Water and dissolved substances can pass between cells and capillaries through the thin capillary walls.

Veins Blood from the capillaries drains into wider tubes called veins. It returns to the heart at low pressure. Some veins contain one-way valves to stop the blood flowing backwards.

The heart

The heart is really two separate pumps in one. One pump sends blood through capillaries in the lungs, where it absorbs oxygen. The other pump takes in this oxygen-carrying blood and pumps it round the rest of the body. The cells use up the oxygen.

Circulation of the blood

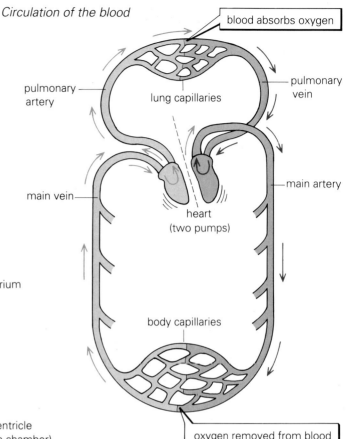

Heart

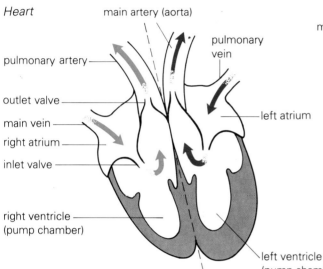

Each pump has two valves. These let blood through in one direction only. Between the valves is a chamber called a **ventricle**. When muscles around the chamber contract, it gets smaller, and blood is pushed out through the outlet valve. When the muscles relax again, more blood flows into the ventricle through the inlet valve.

The muscle contractions are called **beats**. They are set off by nerve impulses produced in the heart itself. However the beat rate can be changed by the nervous system. If you are exercising, your heart beats faster so that your muscles get oxygen more quickly.

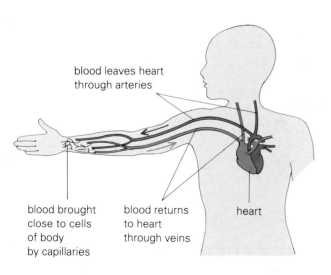

1 *Veins* and *arteries* carry blood. Which of these carry blood a) away from the heart b) back to the heart?
2 What are *capillaries*? What job do they do?
3 Why do the cells of the body need to be close to a supply of blood?
4 What is the liquid part of blood called?
5 Which blood cells help your body fight disease?
6 Which blood cells carry oxygen? What substance is used to carry oxygen?
7 Where does blood absorb oxygen?
8 Why does the heart need valves?
9 Describe what happens to blood as it leaves the pulmonary artery and circulates round the body, back to where it started.

Lungs, liver, and kidneys

By the end of this spread, you should be able to:
• describe the jobs done by the lungs, liver and kidneys
• explain how these organs affect the blood.

Blood supplies the cells of the body with the things they need, and it carries away their waste products. Many substances are carried by the blood, but they have to be kept in the right proportions. This job is partly done by the lungs, liver, and kidneys.

The lungs

When cells of the body respire, they use up oxygen. At the same time, they make carbon dioxide and water. The job of the lungs is to put oxygen into the blood, and remove the unwanted carbon dioxide.

The lungs are two spongy bags of tissue. They are filled with millions of tiny air spaces, called **alveoli**. These have very thin walls, and are surrounded by a network of blood capillaries. Oxygen in the air can seep through these walls and into the blood. At the same time, carbon dioxide (and some water) can seep from the blood into the air.

As you breathe in and out, some of the old air in your lungs is replaced by new, and the **exchange** of oxygen and carbon dioxide takes place.

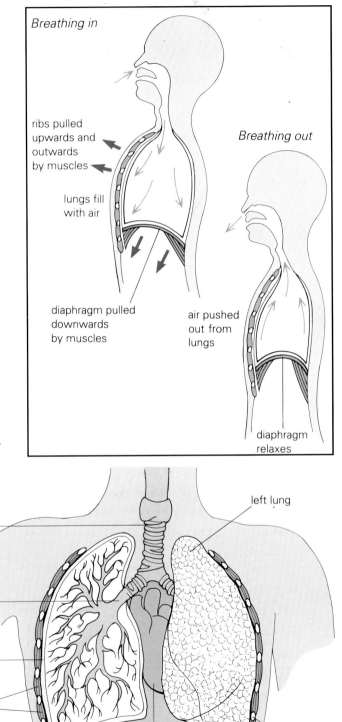

Breathing in

ribs pulled upwards and outwards by muscles

Breathing out

lungs fill with air

diaphragm pulled downwards by muscles

air pushed out from lungs

diaphragm relaxes

blood capillaries

trachea (windpipe)

left lung

right bronchus

pleural cavity

intercostal muscles

air space

alveoli

heart

diaphragm (sheet of muscle)

ribs

Liver

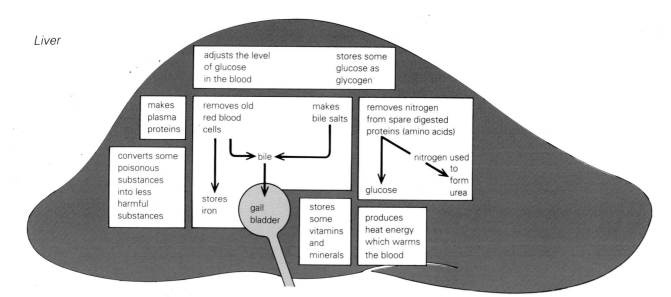

adjusts the level of glucose in the blood

stores some glucose as glycogen

makes plasma proteins

removes old red blood cells

makes bile salts

removes nitrogen from spare digested proteins (amino acids)

nitrogen used to form urea

glucose

converts some poisonous substances into less harmful substances

stores iron

bile

gall bladder

stores some vitamins and minerals

produces heat energy which warms the blood

The liver

The liver is the largest organ in the body. It is a complicated chemical factory with many jobs to do. One of these is to keep you blood topped up with the right amount of 'fuel', **glucose**, for your body cells.

The kidneys

The kidneys 'clean' your blood by filtering it. First, they remove water and other substances. Then they put some of these back so that the proportions are correct. Unwanted water and other substances collect in your bladder as **urine**.

The kidneys are called organs of **excretion** because they remove unwanted substances from your body. The lungs work as organs of excretion as well.

Kidney

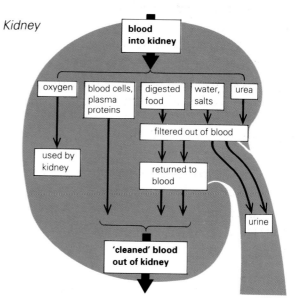

blood into kidney

oxygen | blood cells, plasma proteins | digested food | water, salts | urea

filtered out of blood

used by kidney

returned to blood

urine

'cleaned' blood out of kidney

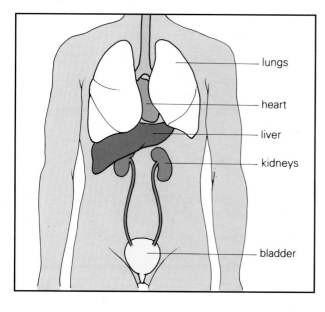

lungs
heart
liver
kidneys
bladder

1 In the lungs:
    a) what substance is taken into the body?
    b) what substance is removed from the body?
2 Why are the tiny air spaces in the lungs surrounded by blood capillaries?
3 What makes your lungs expand when you breathe in?
4 Name *three* things which the liver stores.
5 Descibe *two* other jobs done by the liver.
6 What job is done by the kidneys?
7 What happens to waste substances removed by the kidneys?
8 Why are the kidneys called organs of *excretion*?
9 Give another example of an organ of excretion.

Making human life

By the end of this spread, you should be able to:
- *explain the meaning of ovulation, menstruation, menstrual cycle, and fertilization*
- *describe some methods of birth control.*

A baby grows from a tiny cell in its mother. This cell is formed when an **ovum** (egg) inside the mother is fertilized by a **sperm** from the father.

Puberty is the start of the time when a girl is able to become a mother and a boy to become a father. It often happens around the age of twelve to fourteen, but it is quite normal for it to be earlier or later than this. Girls usually reach puberty before boys.

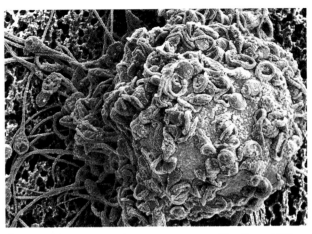

Sperms cluster round an ovum: magnification x500

The female sex system

> **Ovulation** About every 28 days, a woman releases an ovum from one of her **ovaries**. This is called **ovulation**. The tiny ovum moves down the **oviduct** (egg tube) and into the **uterus** (womb).

> **Lining growth** Near the time of ovulation, the lining of the uterus thickens, and a network of blood capillaries grows in it. The uterus is now ready to receive and nourish a fertilized ovum.

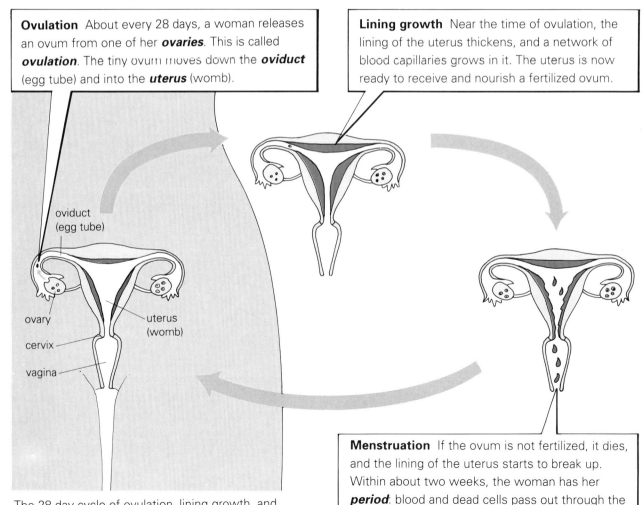

> **Menstruation** If the ovum is not fertilized, it dies, and the lining of the uterus starts to break up. Within about two weeks, the woman has her **period**: blood and dead cells pass out through the vagina. This is called **menstruation**.

The 28-day cycle of ovulation, lining growth, and menstruation is called the **menstrual cycle**.

The male sex system

A man makes sperms in his **testicles**.

Before sperms leave his body, they are mixed with a liquid which comes from glands. Sperms and liquid are called **semen**.

Semen leaves the penis through the same tube as urine.

Fertilization

When a man and woman have sex, the man's penis goes stiff and is placed in the woman's vagina. When the man **ejaculates**, a small amount of semen is pumped from his penis. The semen contains millions of sperms. Some pass into the uterus. And some reach the oviducts, where they may meet an ovum. Only one sperm can fertilize the ovum. After fertilization, an extra 'skin' forms round the ovum to keep out other sperms.

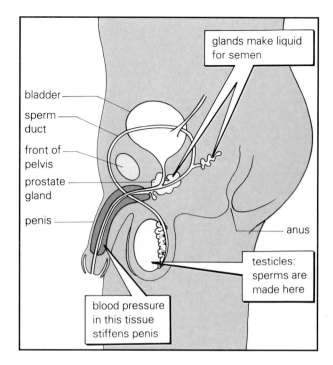

glands make liquid for semen

bladder

sperm duct

front of pelvis

prostate gland

penis

anus

testicles: sperms are made here

blood pressure in this tissue stiffens penis

Birth control

Parents like to give their children the best possible chance in life. For this reason, they may decide to limit the number of children they have. Here are some methods of **contraception** (birth control):

The condom is a thin rubber cover which is put over the man's penis. It traps sperms. A condoms is more reliable if used with a **spermicide**. This is a cream containing chemicals which kills sperms.

The diaphragm is a rubber cover which is put over the woman's cervix. It too stops sperms reaching the uterus. Like a condom, it is best used with a spermicide.

The pill has to be swallowed daily by the woman. It contains chemicals which stop the ovaries releasing ova (eggs). The method is very reliable, but it can cause heart, liver, and breast disease.

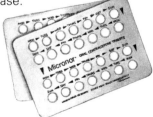

The rhythm method The couple avoids having sex near the time of the month when ovulation is likely. The method is not very reliable, but it can be used by people who think it is wrong to use other kinds of birth control.

---

1 Explain what each of the following means:
   ovum   ovulation   menstrual cycle
2 About how often is an ovum released?
3 What happens to an ovum after it is released, if it is not fertilized?
4 What must happen to an ovum for it to be fertilized?

5 Where are sperms produced?
6 Some methods of contraception are called *barrier* methods because they stop sperms reaching the uterus. Which of the methods shown on this page are barrier methods?
7 What are the disadvantages of a) the pill b) the rhythm method?

Growing to be born

By the end of this spread, you should be able to:
- describe how a fertilized human egg develops into a baby
- describe how a baby is born
- describe some of the factors that can affect the health of an unborn baby.

actual sizes

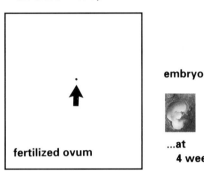

fertilized ovum

embryo

...at 4 weeks

...at 7 weeks

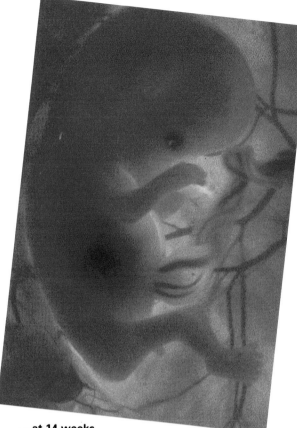

... at 14 weeks

From egg to embryo

An ovum (egg) is a single cell. So is a sperm. When a sperm fertilizes an ovum, the nucleus of the sperm joins with the nucleus of the ovum to become a single nucleus. This now has a full set of chemical instructions to 'build' a baby by cell division.

The fertilized ovum divides over and over again as it passes down the oviduct (egg tube) and into the uterus. As more and more cells are produced, they form a tiny **embryo**. This sinks into to the thick lining of the uterus. The embryo now starts to develop into a baby. The woman is **pregnant**.

The growing embryo

After six weeks, the embryo has a pumping heart, and a brain. It lies in a 'bag' of watery liquid which protects it from jolts and bumps.

The embryo cannot eat and breath, so it must get all the substances it needs from its mother's body. It does this through an organ called the **placenta** which grows into the uterus lining. The embryo is linked to the placenta by an **umbilical cord**.

In the placenta, a thin membrane (sheet) separates the embryo's blood from the mother's. The two blood systems do not mix. But dissolved materials can pass from one to the other across the membrane.

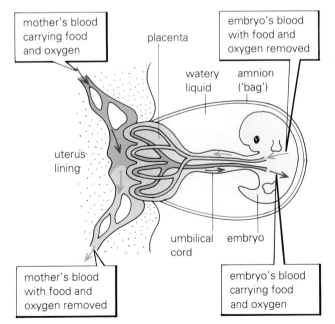

mother's blood carrying food and oxygen

placenta

embryo's blood with food and oxygen removed

watery liquid

amnion ('bag')

uterus lining

umbilical cord

embryo

mother's blood with food and oxygen removed

embryo's blood carrying food and oxygen

Through the placenta, the embryo gets food and oxygen from its mother. Also, carbon dioxide and other waste products are taken away.

Birth

Once an embryo begins to look like a tiny baby, it is called a **foetus**. Birth usually happens about 9 months after fertilization.

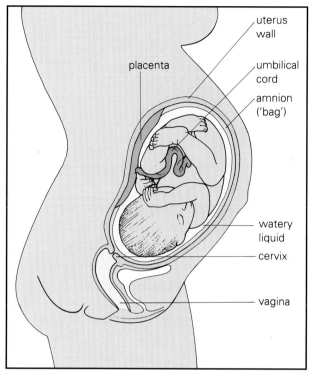

A few days before birth, the baby normally turns so that its head is by the **cervix** (the uterus entrance). As birth approaches, muscles in the walls of the uterus begin to make rhythmic contractions and the cervix starts to open. When the opening is wide enough, the baby's head passes into the vagina. At about this time, the 'bag' bursts and the watery liquid runs out.

---

1 Why must an ovum be fertilized before it can develop into a baby?
2 How is an unborn baby protected from jolts and bumps?
3 Explain what these are: *placenta, umbilical cord*.
4 How does an unborn baby get its food and oxygen?
5 How does an unborn baby get rid of its waste products?
6 How does the position of an unborn baby change a few days before birth? Why?
7 Why is it important that a pregnant mother does not drink alcohol or smoke?

Powerful contractions push the baby from the uterus and out of the mother. Shortly after the birth, more contractions push out the placenta (the 'afterbirth').

The baby gives a loud cry as its lungs fill with air for the first time. From now on, it must take in its own oxygen and food. Soon after birth, the umbilical cord is clipped and cut. Later, the remains of the cord will shrivel away to leave the navel ('belly button').

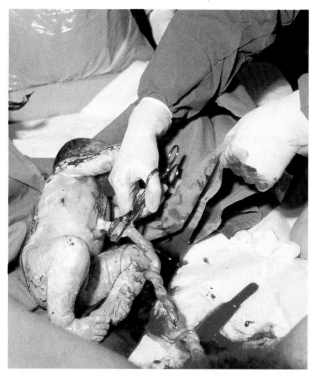

A healthy baby

Care of a baby must start long before it is born. There are many things which can threaten the health of an unborn child:

Smoking Pregnant mothers who smoke tend to have smaller babies than non-smokers. Babies born underweight have more of a struggle for survival.

Alcohol If a pregnant mother drinks alcohol, this can affect the development of her baby. Also, the baby may be premature (born too early).

AIDS Some diseases can be passed from a mother to her unborn baby. AIDS is one example.

German Measles (rubella) If a mother catches German Measles during the first twelve of pregnancy, it can cause deafness, blindness, and heart disease in the baby. That is why girls are given injections to stop them catching German Measles later.

Microbes and health

By the end of this spread, you should be able to:
- *explain how microbes cause and spread disease*
- *describe some of the body's defences against disease*
- *describe the effect of AIDS and how the virus (HIV) can be spread*

Microbes

Microbes are tiny organisms which can only be seen with a microscope. There are billions of them in air, soil, and water, and in our bodies. Some do useful jobs, but some are harmful. Harmful microbes are called **germs**. Most diseases are caused by germs. There are three main types of microbe:

Bacteria are living cells. If the conditions are right, they can multiply very rapidly by cell division. If harmful bacteria invade the body, they attack tissues or release poisons. They are the cause of sore throats as well as more serious diseases such as whooping cough, cholera, and typhoid.

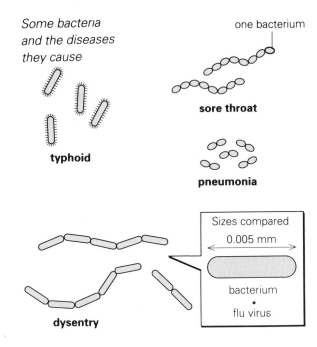

Viruses are much smaller than bacteria. Harmful viruses can invade living cells and upset the way they work. They are responsible for diseases such as flu, chicken-pox, and colds.

Fungi include moulds such as those which grow on old bread. Some skin diseases are caused by fungi, for example: athlete's foot and ringworm.

Spreading germs

Diseases caused by germs are called **infections**. Here are some of the ways in which they can spread:

Droplets in the air When you cough or sneeze, droplets of moisture are sprayed into the air. They carry germs which are breathed in by other people. Colds and flu are spread in this way.

Contact Some diseases can be picked up by touching an infected person. Measles is one example.

Animals Insects can leave germs on food. Blood-sucking insects such as mosquitoes put germs in the blood when they bite. Malaria is spread in this way, by one type of mosquito.

Contaminated food Sewage is full of germs. If it gets into the water supply, food and drink may be affected. Also, people may contaminate food if they have dirty hands which are covered with germs.

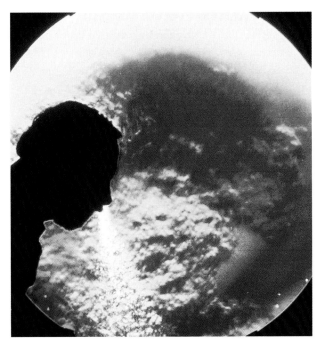

A violent sneeze. To take this photograph, a special technique was used so that air disturbances are seen as different shades and colours.

Fighting disease

Your skin stops some germs from entering the body. However your body has an **immune system** for fighting invaders which do get in. Its 'soldiers' are your white blood cells. Some digest germs. Others make chemicals called **antibodies** which kill them.

Different antibodies are needed for different germs. But fortunately your immune system has a memory. Once it has made antibodies of one type, it can make more of them very quickly if there is another invasion. Once you have had, say, chicken-pox, you are unlikely to get it again. You have become **immune** to the disease. Unfortunately it is almost impossible to become immune to flu and colds. The germs keep changing, and there are many different types.

The body can be given extra help to fight disease:

Antibiotics are medicines which kill bacteria. However, they have no effect on viruses.

Vaccines contain dead or harmless germs which are similar to harmful ones. They are often given by injection. They make the immune system produce antibodies, so that the body's defences are ready if the proper disease ever attacks.

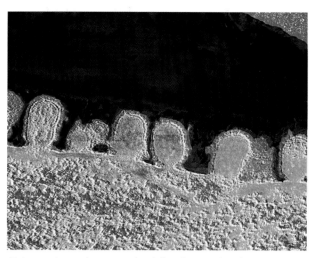

False colour photograph of flu viruses leaving an infected cell: magnification x27000

Healthy living

To help your health, you need to eat sensibly, take plenty of exercise, and avoid health risks:

Poor diet People can run short of vitamins because they do not eat enough fruit and vegetables. Too little fibre in the diet can cause constipation and bowel disease. Too much fat makes you overweight and may lead to heart disease.

Smoking Smoking causes heart attacks, blocked arteries, lung cancer, and breathing difficulties.

Alcohol Years of heavy drinking can damage the liver, heart, and stomach.

Drugs Drugs make people feel excited or relaxed. But some are addictive: the body becomes dependent upon them. Many addicts die before they are 30.

Solvents Sniffing solvents is very dangerous. The vapours damage the lungs and brain.

■■■ AIDS ■■■

AIDS stands for **Acquired Immune Deficiency Syndrome**. It is a disease for which there is no known cure.

AIDS is caused by a virus called **HIV**. People with the virus are **HIV positive**. However, it may be many years before the full disease develops.

HIV attacks white blood cells, so the immune system stops working. AIDS sufferers lose their defence against even mild diseases. Minor illnesses can kill them.

There are only three ways in which AIDS can be passed from one person to another:

- by sexual contact
- by blood-to-blood contact
- from an infected mother to her unborn child.

If a man wears a condom while having sex, this reduces the chances of HIV passing between him and his partner.

1. Give *three* ways in which germs can be passed from one person to another.
2. Why is it important to wash your hands after going to the toilet?
3. How does your body deal with invading germs?
4. What are *vaccines* and what do they do?
5. List some of the things you should do (or *not* do) if you want to stay as healthy as possible.
6. How does AIDS affect the immune system?
7. There are only three ways in which HIV can be passed on. What are they?

Microbes at work

By the end of this spread, you should be able to:
- *explain why food rots, and how the process can be slowed down or stopped*
- *describe how microbes and enzymes are used in the dairy, brewing, and baking industries*

Some microbes are harmful. They make food rot and can threaten our health. But others are helpful. Without microbes, there would be no cheese, yogurt, beer, or wine. And the dough would not rise when bread is made.

Rotting food

Our food can supply microbes with the things they need for their food! If food is left about, it is attacked by microbes (bacteria and fungi). The microbes produce enzymes which **decompose** the food: they break it down into simpler substances. Many of these substances are unpleasant or poisonous.

This fruit is over two months old

Preserving food

Most microbes need air, water, and warmth to grow and multiply. To preserve food, you have to slow down or stop the rotting process. One way of doing this is to kill the microbes, with heat for example. Other ways are removing air or water, or keeping the food in a refrigerator or freezer.

Food may be safely preserved in the supermarket, but things can still go wrong in the kitchen. If meat isn't cooked properly, microbes can quickly multiply and you may end up with food poisoning. If food stays warm and uncovered, this too makes it easier for microbes to multiply.

Killing microbes	Taking away air	Taking away water (liquid)	Lowering the temperature
Pasteurizing *milk is heated to 60 °C to kill harmful microbes, then cooled quickly* Sterilizing *liquid is boiled, or chemicals are used*	Bottling Canning *foods may also be heat treated* Vacuum packing	Drying Freezing *turns water solid* Salting Sugaring Pickling *these draw out water*	Refrigerating Freezing

Dairy food

Not all microbes turn food into nasty substances. Sometimes, the result can be very pleasant to eat. Cheese and yogurt are made by microbes, or by enzymes taken from microbes. The starter material for these foods is milk.

Cheese Milk already has microbes in it. They make it go sour and lumpy. The lumpy bits are called **curds**, and adding an enzyme called **rennin** makes them form more quickly. Curds can be changed into cheese by putting in more microbes. Different microbes can be added later to give the cheese blue 'veins', or holes (gas bubbles).

Yogurt To make yogurt, an enzyme is added to milk. It changes sugar in the milk to lactic acid. This makes the milk go thick and slightly sour.

1 Sometimes microbes can be *harmful*, sometimes they can be *useful*. Give *two* examples of each.
2 Give *two* reasons why freezing preserves food.
3 Why is it important to defrost a chicken thoroughly before cooking it?
4 Why it important to cover leftovers, and put them in the fridge as soon as possible?
5 How does the dairy industry use microbes?
6 What is *fermentation* and what is it used for?
7 Why are there lots of tiny holes in bread?
8 What are *enzymes* and what do they do. (For a full answer to this question you may need to look back to spread 2.5.)

Making alcohol

Yeast cells: magnification x3500. Some of the cells are 'budding'. They are about to form new cells.

Yeast is a single-celled fungus. So yeast is made up of microbes. Yeast has several useful enzymes in it. One of these can make the alcohol in wine:

Grape juice contains lots of natural glucose (a type of sugar). An enzyme in yeast can change this into **ethanol** (often called **alcohol**):

$$\text{glucose} \xrightarrow{\text{enzyme}} \text{ethanol} + \text{carbon dioxide}$$

This process is called **fermentation**. As it takes place, the grape juice froths as carbon dioxide gas is given off. Slowly, the sugary grape juice is turned into wine with alcohol.

Beer is also made by fermentation. But the starter materials are grain and sugar, rather than grapes.

Making bread

Yeast is also used in breadmaking.

Dough is a mixture of flour, water, and yeast. The yeast causes slight fermentation, and the bubbles of carbon dioxide gas make the dough swell up. That is why most of the bread you buy is full of tiny holes.

The variety of life

By the end of this spread, you should be able to:

- *explain how living things on Earth can be classified by their common features*
- *use a key to identify some organisms*

Scientists think that all living things on Earth are related. To show how closely they are related, they try to put them into groups with similar features. They start by grouping them into **kingdoms**. You can see these in the chart on the opposite page.

Humans belong to a large group of animals called the **chordates**. The chordates shown on the chart are known as **vertebrates** because they all have backbones. Here is some information about them:

Fish live in water. They have gills for breathing, scales, and fins.

Amphibians have moist skin. They have lungs, and can live in water and on land. They usually lay their eggs in water.

Reptiles have dry, scaly skin. Most live on land. They lay eggs with a tough leathery skin.

Birds have feathers, and keep a constant body temperature. They lay eggs.

Mammals have hairy skin. They keep a constant body temperature. Most have live young, rather than eggs. The young are fed on milk from the mother.

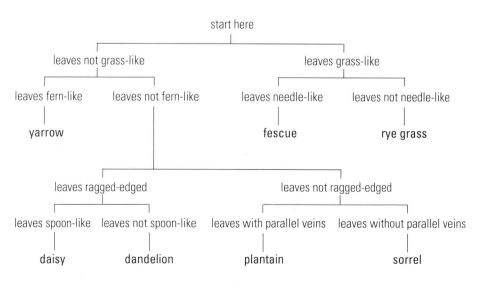

1 In the chart on the right, which animals are *vertebrates*? What do they have in common?
2 Which of the chordates lay eggs?
3 What features do all birds have in common?
4 Where would humans be on the chart? Why?
5 Use the key below to identify the plants above.

Using keys

To help people identify organisms, scientists sometimes construct charts called **keys**. The example on the right is called a **branching key**. You can use it to find the names of the plants in the pictures at the top of the page. For each plant, read the descriptions, follow the route which is the best match, and see where you end up!

start here

leaves not grass-like | leaves grass-like

leaves fern-like | leaves not fern-like | leaves needle-like | leaves not needle-like

yarrow | | fescue | rye grass

leaves ragged-edged | leaves not ragged-edged

leaves spoon-like | leaves not spoon-like | leaves with parallel veins | leaves without parallel veins

daisy | dandelion | plantain | sorrel

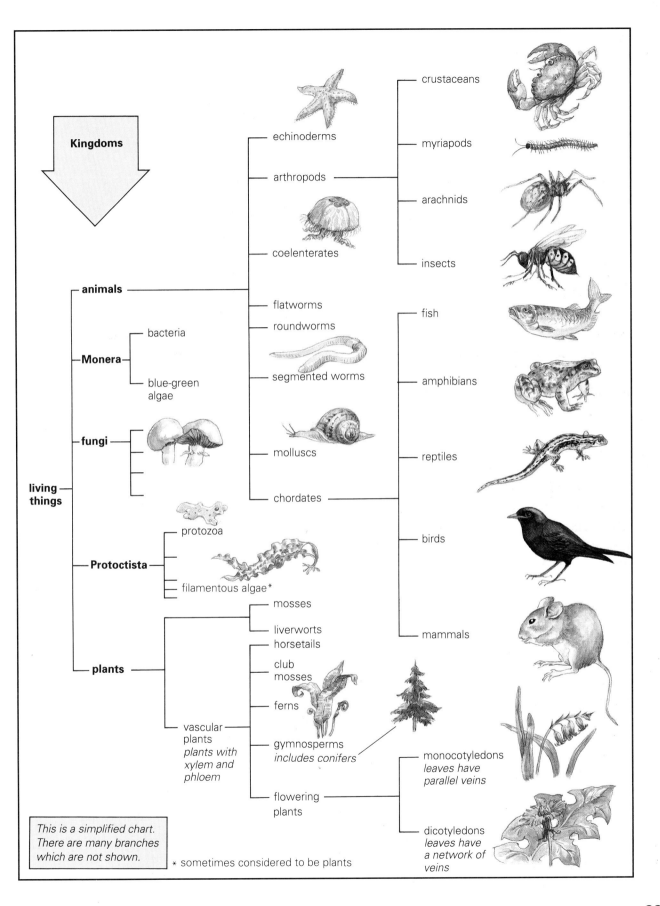

Kingdoms

living things

- **animals**
  - echinoderms
  - arthropods
    - crustaceans
    - myriapods
    - arachnids
    - insects
  - coelenterates
  - flatworms
  - roundworms
  - segmented worms
  - molluscs
  - chordates
    - fish
    - amphibians
    - reptiles
    - birds
    - mammals
- **Monera**
  - bacteria
  - blue-green algae
- **fungi**
- **Protoctista**
  - protozoa
  - filamentous algae*
- **plants**
  - mosses
  - liverworts
  - vascular plants
    plants with xylem and phloem
    - horsetails
    - club mosses
    - ferns
    - gymnosperms
      includes conifers
    - flowering plants
      - monocotyledons
        leaves have parallel veins
      - dicotyledons
        leaves have a network of veins

This is a simplified chart. There are many branches which are not shown.

* sometimes considered to be plants

Pass it on

By the end of this spread, you should be able to:
- *describe how organisms show variation*
- *describe how characteristics depend on genes and on the environment*
- *explain some uses of selective breeding*

Varying features

Your different features are called your **characteristics**. Some, like eye colour, are easy to see. Others, like your blood group, are not so obvious. Many of your characteristics are passed on to you by your parents. They are **inherited**.

No two people are exactly alike. Characteristics like height, weight, and eye and skin colour show **variation**. Identical twins are more alike than most. But even they are not *exactly* alike, as you can see in the photograph.

Continuous variation Humans can be short, or tall, or any height in between. Height shows continuous variation.

Discontinuous variation Some people can roll their tongues, others can't. There is nothing in between. This is an example of discontinuous variation.

All organisms show variation, not just humans.

Genes

A complicated set of chemical instructions is needed to build a human body. Nearly every cell in your body has these instructions. They are stored in the nucleus, in 23 pairs of thread-like **chromosomes**. Small sections of these chromosomes are called **genes**. You have over 100 000 genes altogether. Each gene carries the chemical instructions for a different characteristic.

Genes normally work in pairs. One gene in each pair is inherited from each parent. For example, you may have inherited a gene for black hair from your mother, and a gene for blond hair from your father. Only one of these genes can control your hair colour. A black hair gene is **dominant** over a blond hair gene, so you end up with black hair.

Human cell

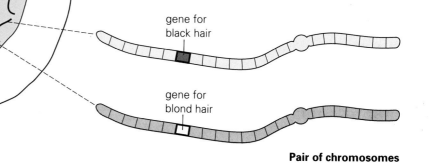

nucleus
containing 46
chromosomes
(23 pairs)

gene for
black hair

gene for
blond hair

Pair of chromosomes

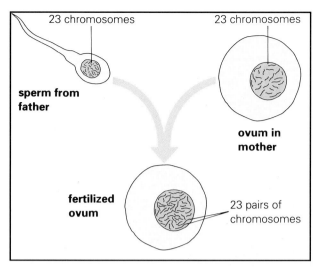

23 chromosomes   23 chromosomes

sperm from father

ovum in mother

fertilized ovum

23 pairs of chromosomes

Each of your parents also inherited *two* genes for each characteristic. However they only passed on *one* of the two to you. It was a matter of chance which one. Unlike other cells, sperms and ova only carry one gene from each pair. But when a sperm combines with an ovum, they make a new cell with a full set of genes. When an ovum is fertilized, millions of gene combinations are possible. That is partly why people can vary so much, even in the same family.

Genes and the environment

Identical twins inherit exactly the same set of genes. Yet one may be heavier than the other because he or she eats more. So, your characteristics depend partly on your genes and partly on your **environment** (your conditions and surroundings). This is true for other organisms as well. For example, two plants may have the same genes. But one may grow better than the other because it has more light, or a better supply of water and minerals from the soil.

1 Give *two* examples of *continuous variation*.
2 Give *two* examples of *discontinuous variation*.
3 What are *genes*? Where are they in your body?
4 Genes are in pairs. Where do the genes in each pair come from?
5 What makes 'identical' twins look alike?
6 Why are 'identical' twins not exactly alike?
7 Give *two* examples of the use of selective breeding.
8 Why is it important to preserve rare breeds of animal or rare varieties of plants?

Selective breeding

People often try to breed animals with special characteristics: for example, sheep with plenty of wool, or horses that can run fast. To do this, they select the animals which will be mated. This is called *selective breeding*. The idea is that the offspring ('babies') may inherit the best features of both parents. But chance still affects the result. If two champion racehorses mate, their offspring will not necessarily be a champion.

Selective breeding is also used with plants. For example, one variety of wheat may grow faster than another, or be more resistant to disease. By controlling how the wheat is pollinated, scientists can breed varieties with the characteristics they want. This helps give larger crops (bigger **yields**).

Saving genes

Sometimes, a type of animal or plant may completely die out. It may become **extinct**. Once an organism is extinct, its genes are lost for ever.

Farmers try to preserve rare breeds of farm animal in order to save their genes. If disease strikes a common breed, all the animals might die. However, if a rare breed has genes which make it resistant to the disease, it can be used to improve the first breed.

Dartmoor Greyface Sheep from the Cotswold Farm Park, Gloucestershire.

Living together

By the end of this spread, you should be able to:
- *describe some of the factors which affect living things and their environment*
- *explain how living things are adapted to their environment*

The place where an animal or plant lives is called its **habitat**. It is usually a habitat for other animals and plants as well. All the living things in one habitat are called a **community**. Their **environment** is everything around them which affects their way of life. Together, a community and its environment are known as an **ecosystem**.

Here are some of the factors which affect an organism's environment:

---

1 Explain what these words mean:
   habitat   population   community   predator
2 Give an example of how an animal's environment can change from one part of the day to another.
3 Give an example of how a plant's environment can change from season to another.
4 How do plants compete with each other?
5 If an animal is *adapted to its environment*, what does this mean? Give an example.
6 In the graph on the opposite page a) why does the slug population fall? b) why does it then start to rise again?
7 What would happen to the number of toads if a chemical killed off half of the plants? Why?

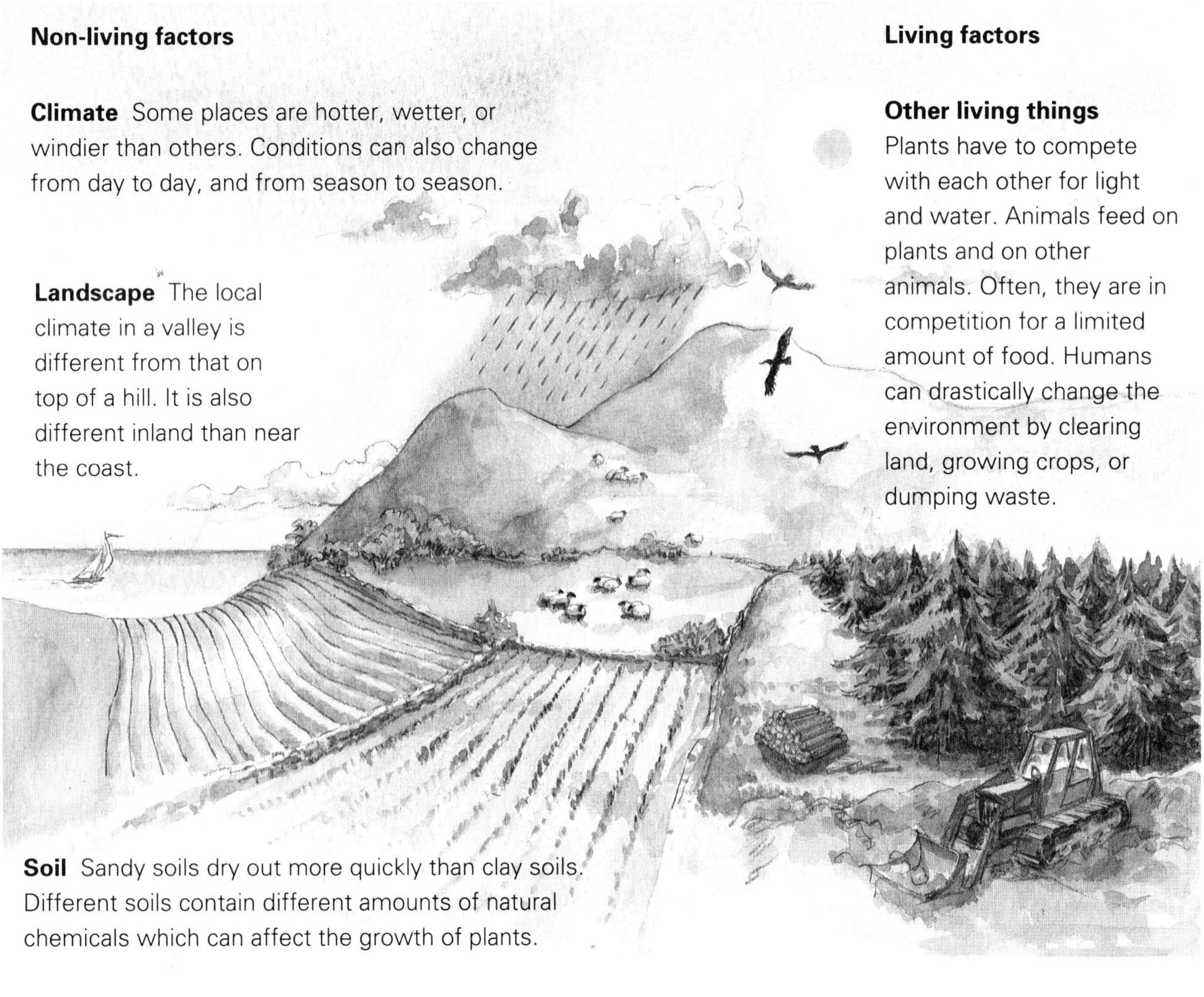

Non-living factors

Climate Some places are hotter, wetter, or windier than others. Conditions can also change from day to day, and from season to season.

Landscape The local climate in a valley is different from that on top of a hill. It is also different inland than near the coast.

Soil Sandy soils dry out more quickly than clay soils. Different soils contain different amounts of natural chemicals which can affect the growth of plants.

Living factors

Other living things Plants have to compete with each other for light and water. Animals feed on plants and on other animals. Often, they are in competition for a limited amount of food. Humans can drastically change the environment by clearing land, growing crops, or dumping waste.

Adapted for living

Over many millions of years, animals and plants have developed special features to help them cope with their way of life. They have become **adapted** to their environment. Here are some examples:

- Dormice and many other small mammals hibernate in the winter months so that they can survive when food is scarce. They go to sleep with their life processes slowed right down.
- Hawks have claws and a beak which are specially shaped for gripping small animals and tearing them apart.
- Many trees lose their leaves in the autumn. This means that they do not need to take up so much water during the months when the ground might be frozen.

Adapted for hunting. The chameleon has a long tongue which it can flick out to catch insects

Changing populations

A group of animals of the same kind is called a **population**. Animals depend on plants or other animals for their food. So a change in one population may affect several other populations.

Animals which feed on other animals are known as **predators**. The animals that they eat are called their **prey**.

Imagine a garden with a stream running through it. This is a habitat for toads, slugs, and plants. The toads feed on the slugs, and the slugs feed on the plants. Normally, the numbers of toads, slugs, and plants will reach a balance. The graphs show what happens if too many toads start to develop. Over a period of time, the balance is restored.

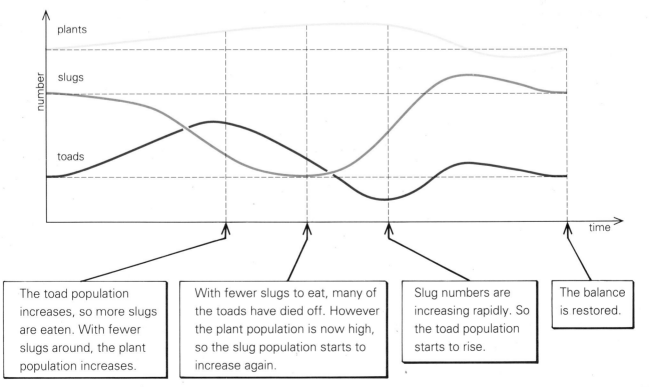

The toad population increases, so more slugs are eaten. With fewer slugs around, the plant population increases.

With fewer slugs to eat, many of the toads have died off. However the plant population is now high, so the slug population starts to increase again.

Slug numbers are increasing rapidly. So the toad population starts to rise.

The balance is restored.

Populations and pollution

By the end of this spread, you should be able to:
* *describe problems caused by the demand for food and materials*
* *describe how human activities cause different types of pollution*

The world's human population is growing. As it does so, it needs more crops, meat, wood, fuels, and minerals. This is causing problems for other populations, and for humans as well:

Using fertilizers To help crops grow, chemical fertilizers are often sprayed onto soil. But they can be washed into lakes and rivers, where they encourage the growth of green, plant-like algae. Microbes feeding on dead algae use up all the oxygen in the water, so fish and other organisms die.

Pesticides These are chemicals sprayed onto crops to kill off insects and other pests. But they can build up in the bodies of birds which feed on the pests. And they can also be washed into lakes and rivers.

Cutting down forests Huge areas of forest are being cut down for timber, or to make space for agriculture or industry. But trees supply the world with some of its oxygen. And they provide shelter for many forms of wildlife. When trees are removed, the soil is easily eroded (worn away), and large areas of ground can be turned into desert, or bog if it is wet.

Digging up land Industry needs fuels and other materials from the ground. For example, huge amounts of limestone (above) are needed for making concrete. And limestone is also used in the manufacture of steel and glass. But mining and quarrying damage the landscape. They can also produce huge heaps of waste materials. Some of these contain poisonous metals which can harm plants.

Fishing Fish is an important food for millions of people. But if too many fish are taken from the sea, there are not enough left to breed. Soon, the fish die out altogether.

Crops Farmers find it more efficient to grow single crops in huge fields. But cutting down hedges destroys the habitats for many forms of wildlife. And pests which feed on the one crop can flourish.

Air pollution

Harmful gases When coal, oil, and petrol are burned, the waste gases include sulphur dioxide and nitrogen oxides. Unless removed, these dissolve in rainwater to form *acid rain*. This corrodes steel, eats into stonework, and damages plants.

Carbon dioxide This is the main gas given off when fuels burn. It traps the Sun's heat and causes *global warming* (the *greenhouse effect*).

Dust Dust from quarries, mines, and factories can cause lung disease.

Smoke This contains particles of soot (carbon) which can blacken buildings.

Pollution
This is anything unwanted which humans put into the environment.

Other pollution

Radiation If an accident happens, radioactive waste from a nuclear power station can contaminate the air, sea, and soil.

Noise Noisy aircraft, or someone else's loud radio, can be very annoying.

Litter Some litter rots away: paper for example. But some does not rot: plastic and glass for example. Litter looks awful, and it can cause injury to animals.

Water pollution

Factory waste Poisonous chemicals are sometimes dumped into rivers or the sea.

Fertilizers and pesticides These can get into lakes and rivers and harm wildlife (see opposite page).

Slurry This farm waste is a mixture of animal droppings and urine. It is used as a fertilizer, but can pollute streams and rivers.

Oil This sometimes spills from tankers. It kills sea-birds and marine life. And it ruins beaches.

Sewage is often dumped at sea. It can be a health hazard.

---

1 A *Using fertilizers and pesticides*
   B *Cutting down forests*
   C *Making larger fields*
   D *Quarrying limestone*
   Give *two* reasons for doing each of the above. Then give *two* problems caused by each one.

2 What causes acid rain?

3 What damage does acid rain do?

4 Give *three* examples of how a river might become polluted.

5 Give an example of how our demand for materials might threaten another animal population.

Chains, webs, and pyramids

By the end of this spread, you should be able to:
- explain what food chains and food webs are
- draw pyramids of numbers and biomass
- describe what decomposers are and what they do

Food chains

All living things need food. It supplies them with their energy and the materials they need for building their bodies.

Plants are **producers**. They produce their own food. But animals are **consumers**. They have to get their food by consuming (eating) other living things.

A **food chain** shows how living things feed on other living things. For example, if a blackbird feeds on snails, and these feed on leaves, then the food chain looks like the one on the right.

Pyramid of numbers

In a food chain, only a fraction of the energy taken in by one organism reaches the next. So fewer and fewer organisms can be fed at each stage. For example, it might take 30 000 leaves to feed 300 snails, and 300 snails to feed one blackbird. This can be shown using a **pyramid of numbers** like the one below.

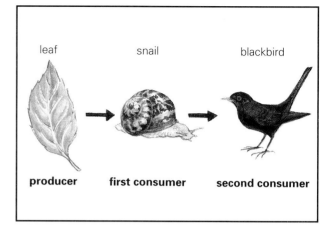

leaf	snail	blackbird
producer	**first consumer**	**second consumer**

A simple food chain

Pyramid of biomass

A leaf is lighter than a snail. So the numbers of leaves and snails do not really give an accurate picture of how much food is being eaten at each stage of the chain. For this, scientists use the idea of **biomass**. In a food chain:

The biomass is the total mass of each type of organism.

The biomasses of the leaves, snails, and bird have been worked out in the table below. Using this information, a **pyramid of biomass** can be drawn.

	A Number	**B** Mass ofeach in g	**A x B** Biomass in g
blackbirds	1	250	250
snails	300	50	15 000
leaves	30 000	20	600 000

(g = gram)

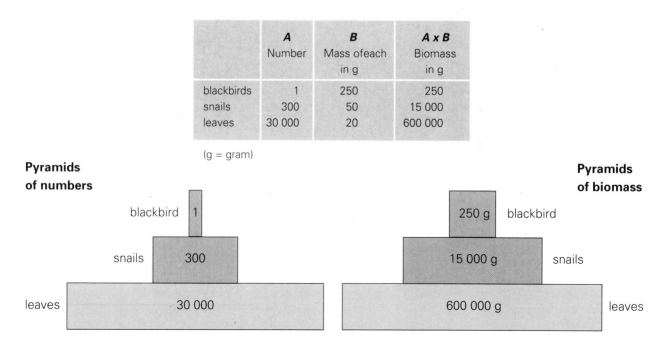

Pyramids of numbers

blackbird 1
snails 300
leaves 30 000

Pyramids of biomass

250 g blackbird
15 000 g snails
600 000 g leaves

Food webs

Many animals eat more than one type of food. So organisms can be part of several food chains. The result is a network of linked food chains called a **food web**. Here is an example:

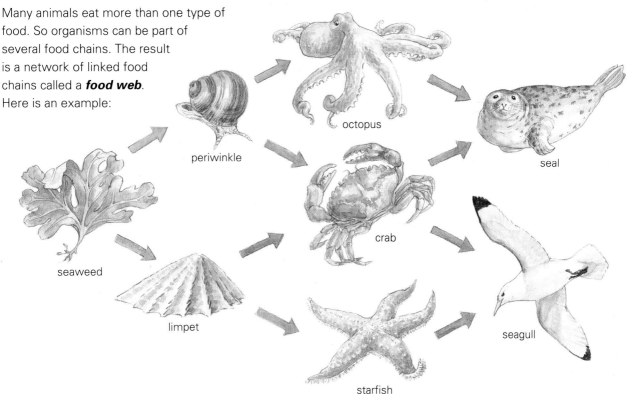

octopus

periwinkle

seaweed

limpet

crab

starfish

seal

seagull

Decomposers at work

Many microbes (bacteria and fungi) feed on the remains of dead plants and animals. They produce enzymes which make the dead things decompose (rot) into a liquid. Then they feed on the liquid.

Microbes which make things rot are known as **decomposers**.

Decomposers are important because:
- they get rid of dead plants and animals
- they put useful chemicals back into the soil.

Materials which rot are called **biodegradable** materials. As well as dead plants and animals, they include things made from plant or animal matter, such as paper, wool, and cotton.

1 What is the difference between a *producer* and a *consumer*? Give an example of each.
2 What are *biodegradable* materials? Give *two* examples?
3 In the food web on this page, what other organisms would be affected if periwinkles were poisoned by chemical waste? Explain what might happen to these organisms.
4 A frog feeds on 250 worms. These feed on 25 000 leaves. Draw the pyramid of numbers.
5 The frog in the last question has a mass of 200 g, a worm 40 g, and a leaf 20 g. Draw the pyramid of biomass. (Hint: start by making a table like the one on the opposite page.)

Recycling atoms

By the end of this spread, you should be able to:
- *explain how atoms of carbon and nitrogen are recycled by living things*

Like everything else, living things are made of **atoms**. These join together in different ways to form different materials in the body. As plants and animals grow and die, most of their atoms are used over and over again.

The carbon cycle

There is a small amount of carbon dioxide in the atmosphere. Plants take in some for photosynthesis, so their bodies are partly carbon. Animals eat plants, so their bodies are partly carbon as well. Respiration puts carbon dioxide back into the atmosphere. So does burning.

As photosynthesis, respiration, and burning take place, carbon atoms are used over and over again. This process is called the **carbon cycle**.

4% carbon
20% carbon
90% carbon

Atoms in living things

Mainly............................ oxygen, carbon, hydrogen
with some......................nitrogen
and smaller amounts of calcium, phosphorus, others

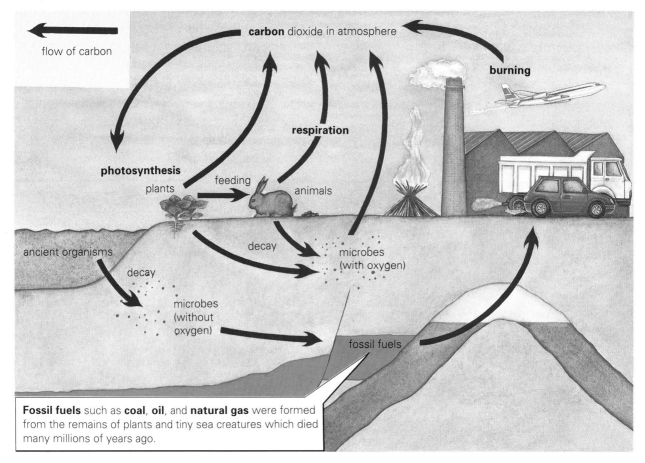

carbon dioxide in atmosphere

flow of carbon

burning

respiration

photosynthesis

plants

feeding

animals

decay

microbes (with oxygen)

ancient organisms

decay

microbes (without oxygen)

fossil fuels

Fossil fuels such as **coal**, **oil**, and **natural gas** were formed from the remains of plants and tiny sea creatures which died many millions of years ago.

The nitrogen cycle

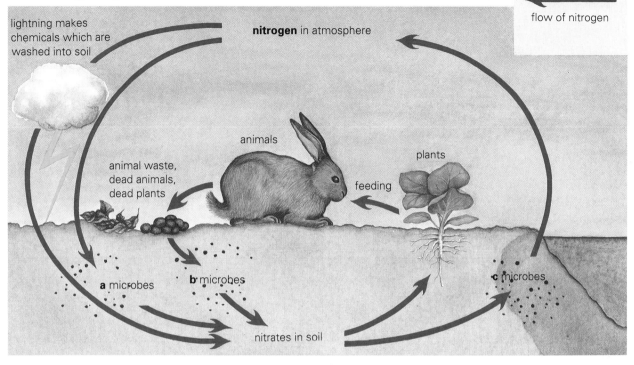

Living things need nitrogen to help make the proteins in their body tissues. There is plenty of nitrogen in the atmosphere, but it is of no direct use to plants or animals because it does not easily take part in chemical changes.

Plants get their nitrogen by taking in chemicals called *nitrates* from the soil. These are partly made from nitrogen. They dissolve easily and are absorbed through roots. Animals get their nitrogen by eating plants (or by eating other animals which have fed on plants).

Nitrogen is used over and over again by living things. The process is called the *nitrogen cycle*. Microbes in the soil have an important part to play:

a Some microbes use nitrogen from the air to make nitrates. They release these into the soil.

b Some microbes make nitrates from animal waste, dead animals, and dead plants.

c Some microbes in wet soil remove nitrogen from nitrates and release it into the atmosphere.

The nodules on the roots of this pea plant contain microbes which take in nitrogen and make nitrates.

1 *Respiration   photosynthesis   burning*
   Which of the above processes takes carbon dioxide from the atmosphere?
2 Which of the above processes put carbon dioxide into the atmosphere?
3 Describe how the carbon atoms in a lump of coal can end up as part of the body of an animal.
4 Why do living things need nitrogen?
5 How do plants get their nitrogen?
6 How do animals get their nitrogen?
7 If plants take nitrates from the soil, how are these nitrates replaced?

3·1 Materials and properties

By the end of this spread, you should be able to:
* *describe how materials can be classified*
* *describe properties which different materials can have*

Solids, liquids, and gases

Materials are either solid, liquid, or gas:

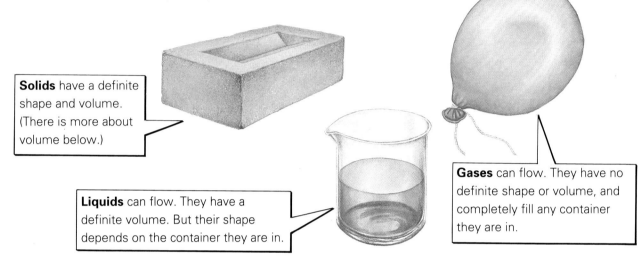

Solids have a definite shape and volume. (There is more about volume below.)

Liquids can flow. They have a definite volume. But their shape depends on the container they are in.

Gases can flow. They have no definite shape or volume, and completely fill any container they are in.

Mass, volume, and density

The amount of matter in something is called its mass. It can be measured in **kilograms (kg)**.

The amount of space something takes up is called its volume. It can be measured in **cubic metres (m^3)**.

A block of steel has a much more mass in every cubic metre than a block of wood. Scientists say that steel has a greater **density** than wood.

Steel has a density of 7800 kg/m^3. This means that there is 7800 kg of mass in each cubic metre. Some other density values are also shown below.

You can calculate density with this equation:

$$density = \frac{mass}{volume}$$

mass in kg
volume in m^3
density in kg/m^3

For example, if a block of coal has a mass of 3200 kg and a volume of 2 m^3, its density is 3200 divided by 2, which is 1600 kg/m^3.

Gases have mass. However, liquids and solids are usually much more dense than gases. For example, the lemonade in a bottle is about 750 times heavier than the air in an empty bottle.

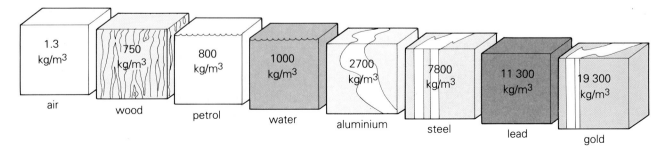

1.3 kg/m^3	750 kg/m^3	800 kg/m^3	1000 kg/m^3	2700 kg/m^3	7800 kg/m^3	11 300 kg/m^3	19 300 kg/m^3
air	wood	petrol	water	aluminium	steel	lead	gold

Densities of different materials

Looking at properties

The features of a material and how it behaves are called its **properties**. Below are some of the words for describing them:

Property	Meaning	Example
Strong	Resists the effects of forces	Steel
Brittle	Hard, but breaks easily	Glass
Malleable	Can be hammered into shape	Copper
Ductile	Can be pulled out into wires	Copper
Transparent	'See-through': lets light through	Glass
Translucent	Lets light through, but scatters it	White polythene
Flexible	Can be bent or twisted without breaking	White polythene
Conductor (heat)	Lets heat pass through easily	Copper
Conductor (electricity)	Lets electricity pass through easily	Copper
Insulator (heat)	Stops heat passing through	Expanded polystyrene
Insulator (electricity)	Stops electricity passing through	PVC

Grouping solids

Here are five important groups of materials used for making things:

Ceramics Brittle materials made by heating clay or similar materials in kilns. They can usually withstand very high temperatures.

Glasses Brittle materials, made partly from sand. They are transparent or translucent, and are good electrical insulators.

Plastics Wide range of chemically-made *(synthetic)* materials. During manufacture, while still warm, they are flexible and can be moulded. Many are also flexible when cold. They melt easily. They are good electrical insulators.

Metals Shiny solids that conduct heat and electricity. They are often malleable and ductile, and difficult to melt.

Fibres Threads made from natural or synthetic materials.

---

1 What are the differences between
   a) a solid and a liquid b) a liquid and a gas?
2 *Water has a density of 1000 kg/m³.*
   a) What does this tell you about the water?
   b) What would be the mass of 5 m³ of water?
3 Why would ceramics not be suitable for making springs?

4 Below, are some jobs to be done by different materials. What *properties* do you think each material should have? (You could use words on this page, or others of your own choosing.)
   a) Window in a greenhouse b) Knife
   c) Bottom of a saucepan d) Handle of a kettle
   e) Covering on an electric wire.

Elements, atoms, and compounds

By the end of this spread, you should be able to:
* *explain what elements and compounds are*
* *describe how some metals are more reactive than others*

Elements

Everything on Earth is made from about 90 simple substances called **elements**. Elements can combine in different ways to form thousands of new substances. For example, water is a combination of the elements hydrogen and oxygen.

There are two main types of element: **metals** and **nonmetals**. Every element has its own chemical symbol. You can see some examples in the table.

Metals These are usually hard and shiny, and difficult to melt. They are good conductors of heat and electricity.

Nonmetals These are usually gases, or solids which melt easily. The solids are often brittle or powdery. Most are insulators.

Carbon has unusual properties for a nonmetal. It exists naturally in two forms: **graphite**, which is a good conductor of electricity, and **diamond**, which is the hardest substance known.

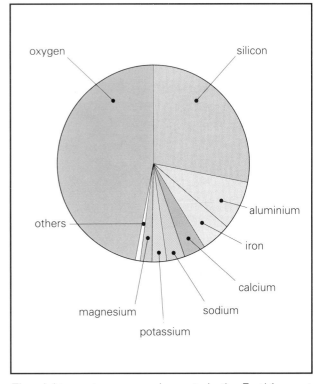

The eight most common elements in the Earth's crust (outer layer). The rocks are mainly made from oxygen and silicon.

Graphite

Diamond

Metals		Nonmetals	
Element	*Symbol*	*Element*	*Symbol*
aluminium	Al	bromine	Br
calcium	Ca	carbon	C
copper	Cu	chlorine	Cl
gold	Au	fluorine	F
iron	Fe	helium	He
lead	Pb	hydrogen	H
magnesium	Mg	iodine	I
potassium	K	nitrogen	N
silver	Ag	oxygen	O
sodium	Na	phosphorus	P
tin	Sn	silicon	Si
zinc	Zn	sulphur	S

Atoms

Elements are made up of tiny particles called **atoms**. An atom is the smallest amount of an element you can have. Atoms are far too small to see with any ordinary microscope. It would take more than a billion billion atoms to cover this full stop.

Different elements have different types of atom. Hydrogen is the lightest atom (see Spread 3.5).

Compounds

Atoms can join together to form a new substance which is quite different from the elements forming it. This new substance is called a **compound**.

Water is a compound of hydrogen and oxygen. The smallest 'bit' of water is called a **molecule** of water. It is made up of two hydrogen atoms stuck to one oxygen atom. Scientists describe it using a **chemical formula**: H_2O.

There are some examples of compounds and formulae on the right. However, not all compounds are in the form of molecules (see Spread 3.8).

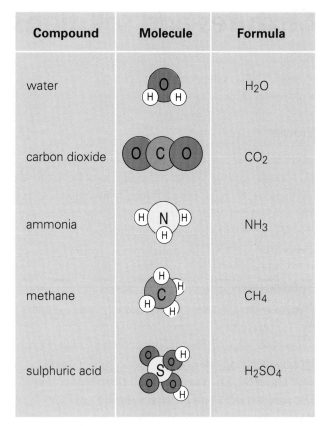

Compound	Molecule	Formula
water		H_2O
carbon dioxide		CO_2
ammonia		NH_3
methane		CH_4
sulphuric acid		H_2SO_4

Reactivity

When elements join, scientists say that they have **reacted** with each other. They have taken part in a **chemical reaction**.

Some metals react more readily than others. For example, iron can react with oxygen to form a compound called **rust**. Because iron reacts so readily, it is never found in the ground as a pure metal. Instead, it has to be extracted from a brown, rusty compound called **haematite**. On the other hand, gold is very unreactive. It is found in rocks as tiny pieces of pure metal.

Scientists have worked out a **reactivity series** for metals. You can see part of this below:

---

1 What are the two main types of element?
2 Which of the eight most common elements in the Earth's crust are metals?
3 Which element has the lightest atoms?
4 What is the difference between an *element* and a *compound*.
5 The chemical formula for carbon dioxide is CO_2. What does this tell you about carbon dioxide?
6 Explain why gold is found in the ground as a pure metal, whereas iron has to be extracted from compounds in rocks.
7 Do you think aluminium is found in the ground as a pure metal? Explain your answer.

---

least reactive ➤ most reactive

Au	Ag	Cu	Pb	Fe	Zn	Al	Mg	Ca	Na	K
gold	silver	copper	lead	iron	zinc	aluminium	magnesium	calcium	sodium	potassium

these metals react with acids

Mixtures and solutions

By the end of this spread, you should be able to:
* *explain what solutions and alloys are.*
* *describe ways of separating mixtures.*

One substance by itself is called a **pure** substance. It might be an element, such as gold, or it might be a compound, such as water. However, very few natural substances are pure. For example, rainwater contains tiny amounts of other chemicals as well. If something contains at least two separate substances, it is called a **mixture**.

Solutions

If you put sand in salt, the particles in the mixture are big enough to see. However, if you put sugar in water, the sugar breaks up into particles which are so small and spread out that you cannot see them even with a microscope. The sugar has **dissolved** in water. The result is a mixture called a **solution**:

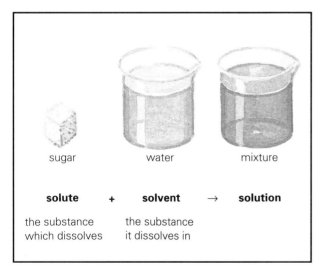

| sugar | water | mixture |

solute + **solvent** → **solution**

| the substance which dissolves | the substance it dissolves in | |

Scientists say that sugar is **soluble** in water.

A solution containing water is called an **aqueous solution**. However water is not the only solvent for dissolving things. Here are some other solvents:

Solvent	Dissolves...
Ethanol	Biro ink
Trichloroethane	Grease
Propanone	Nail varnish

Brass is an alloy

Alloys

Metals with other substances mixed in are called **alloys**.

The instrument above is made of an alloy, brass. Brass is a mixture of copper (70%) and zinc (30%). It is harder than copper by itself. Also, unlike copper, it does not **corrode**. In other words, its surface is not spoilt by the chemical action of air or water.

Steel is an alloy of iron (99%) and carbon (1%). (Exact percentages vary depending on the type of steel). Steel is much stronger and harder than iron by itself.

---

1 What do scientists mean by a *pure* substance?
2 What do these words mean?
   soluble   solute   solvent   solution
3 What is an *alloy*?
4 Metal things are often made from alloys rather than pure metals. Why?
5 Describe how you would separate the substances in each of the following mixtures:
   a) sand and sugar b) water and mud
   c) water paints of different colours.
6 Which of the following work as filters, and what do they separate?
   tea-bag   cotton wool   bag in vacuum cleaner

Separating mixtures

Below are some methods of separating simple mixtures in the laboratory, with examples of what they might be used for:

Filtering

Example Separating sand from water.

The mixture is poured into a funnel lined with filter paper. The water passes through the paper, but the sand is stopped.

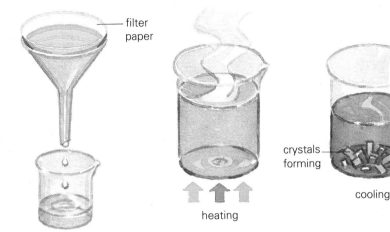

filter paper

crystals forming

cooling

heating

Dissolving

Example Separating sand from salt.

The sand and salt are mixed with water and stirred. This dissolves the salt, but not the sand. The new mixture is filtered. The salty water passes through the filter paper, but the sand is stopped.

Crystallizing

Example Separating copper(II) sulphate from water.

The solution is heated gently and some of the water evaporates. When the remaining solution is cooled, crystals of copper(II) sulphate start to form in it.

salt solution

heat

salt (solid) left behind

heat

spot (ink mixture)

filter paper

water

Evaporating

Example Separating salt from water.

The solution is heated gently until all the water has evaporated (turned to vapour). The salt is left behind as a solid.

Distilling

Example Separating water from ink.

The mixture is boiled. The vapour, which is pure water, cools as it passes down a long tube and condenses (turns liquid).

Chromatography

Example Separating inks of different colours.

A spot of ink mixture is placed at the centre of a piece of filter paper and left to dry. Water is dripped onto the spot. The ink mixture spreads through the damp paper. The different colours spread at different rates.

Acids and bases

By the end of this spread, you should be able to:
- list the main properties of acids and bases
- use the pH scale and explain what it is for
- explain what is meant by neutralization

Acids

There are acids in the laboratory. But there are natural acids in vinegar, sour fruits, and even in your stomach! Acids dissolved in lots of water are called **dilute** acids. The more **concentrated** an acid, the less water it is dissolved in.

Dissolved in water, acids are **corrosive** and eat into materials such as carbonates and some metals. Even without water, some concentrated acids are dangerously corrosive and should never be handled.

All acids contain hydrogen. In water, this becomes active and causes the acid effect. When an acid reacts with a metal, the hydrogen is given off and a new substance called a **salt** is formed. Here is a typical reaction between an acid and a metal:

sulphuric acid + magnesium → magnesium sulphate + hydrogen

In this case, magnesium sulphate is the salt. There are many different types of salt.

Acids which release lots of hydrogen, and dissolve metals quickly, are called **strong acids**. Those which release hydrogen slowly are **weak acids**.

Some naturally-occurring acids

	contains....
lemon juice	citric acid
vinegar	ethanoic acid (acetic acid)
tea	tannic acid
sour milk	lactic acid
grapes	tartaric acid
nettle sting	methanoic acid
stomach (juices)	hydrochloric acid

Strong acids	Weak acids
hydrochloric acid	ethanoic acid
sulphuric acid	citric acid
nitric acid	carbonic acid

Bases

Bases are the chemical 'opposites' of acids. They react strongly with acids and can **neutralize** them (cancel out the acid effect).

Bases which dissolve in water are called **alkalis**. So alkalis are soluble bases.

Alkalis can be just as corrosive as acids. Their powerful chemical action is often used in bath, sink, and oven cleaners.

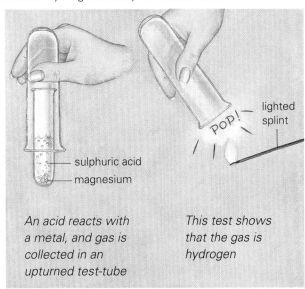

sulphuric acid
magnesium

lighted splint

POP!

An acid reacts with a metal, and gas is collected in an upturned test-tube

This test shows that the gas is hydrogen

Alkalis, including ammonia, are used in many household cleaners

Indicators and pH

There are some dyes which have a different colour depending on whether they are in an acidic or alkaline solution. Dyes like this are called **indicators**. Litmus is one example.

Acids turn litmus red.
Alkalis turn litmus blue.

Scientists use the **pH scale** to measure how strong or weak an acid or alkali is. The strongest acids have a pH of 1. The strongest alkalis have a pH of 14. Solutions with a pH of 7 are are neither acidic nor alkaline. They are **neutral**.

You can measure pH with **universal indicator**. This contains a mixture of dyes. It goes a different colour depending on the pH of the solution.

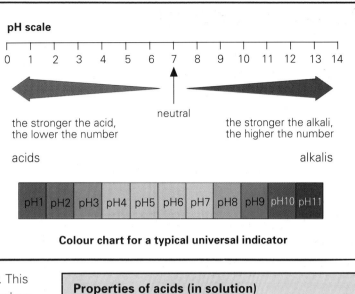

Colour chart for a typical universal indicator

Neutralization

If an acid reacts with a base it can form a neutral solution containing a salt. For example:

hydrochloric acid + sodium hydroxide → sodium chloride + water

In other words:

acid + base → salt + water

Neutralizing acids is called **neutralization**. Here are some everyday examples:

Sugar in your mouth produces acids which rot your teeth. Toothpaste, which is alkaline, neutralizes these acids. Acid in your stomach sometimes becomes a little too concentrated. Indigestion tablets contain an alkali, such as sodium hydrogencarbonate ('bicarb'), which helps reduce the effect.

Properties of acids (in solution)
- They have a sour taste (like vinegar)
  Note: you must never taste laboratory acids
- They turn litmus red
- They usually react with metals, producing hydrogen and a salt
- They dissolve carbonates to give salt, water, and carbon dioxide
- They have pH numbers less than 7

Properties of alkalis (in solution)
- They feel soapy
  Note: it is dangerous to touch laboratory alkalis
- They turn litmus blue
- They have pH numbers greater than 7

Strong alkalis	Weak alkali
sodium hydroxide potassium hydroxide calcium hydroxide	ammonia

1 What is the difference between a *concentrated* acid and a *dilute* acid?
2 What is the difference between a *strong* acid and a *weak* acid?
3 What element is found in all acids?
4 Someone drops some zinc into sulphuric acid and finds that a gas is given off. What gas is it? How could you tell it was this gas by experiment?
5 What is produced if an acid is added to a base?
6 Someone puts some universal indicator paper into vinegar. The pH is 3. What does this tell you about the vinegar?
7 Someone puts some universal indicator paper onto wet soap. The pH is 8. What does this tell you about the soap?
8 What would you expect the pH of pure water to be?
9 Give *two* examples of neutralization.

The periodic table

By the end of this spread, you should be able to:
- *describe the main features of the periodic table*
- *explain why different elements have different properties*

The elements differ in many ways. For example, some have a greater density than others. And some are more reactive than others.

Density is an example of a **physical property**. Reactivity is an example of a **chemical property**.

Scientists have found links between the elements, their properties, and their atoms.

Atoms, electrons, and shells

An atom's mass is mainly concentrated in a tiny **nucleus** in the centre. Around this nucleus, there are even tinier particles called **electrons**.

Each element has a different number of electrons in its atom. Hydrogen, the lightest atom, has only one electron. Uranium, one of the heaviest, has 92.

In an atom, the electrons are arranged in layers called **shells**. For example, the first shell can hold up to 2 electrons, the second up to 8, and the third up to 8. Electrons always try to fill the lowest shell they can. Some elements have full outer shells. But most have outer shells which are only partly filled. You can see some examples in the table on the opposite page.

Properties and patterns

The elements below have been arranged in order of number of electrons. Along the row, you can see that some properties tend to follow a periodic (repeating) pattern:

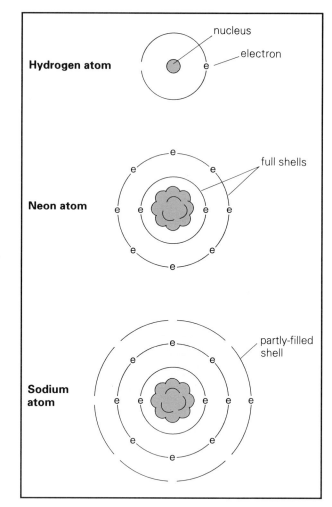

From observations like this scientists have been able to construct a chart of the elements, called the **periodic table**. There is a simple version at the top of the next page, and a full table on page 128. The elements have been arranged in several rows, called **periods**, one on top of another. As a result, elements with similar properties are in the same column.

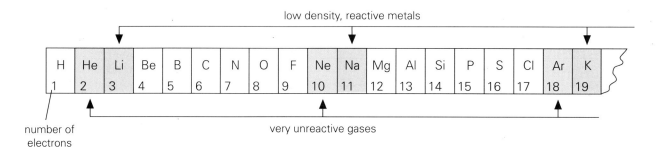

low density, reactive metals

H	He	Li	Be	B	C	N	O	F	Ne	Na	Mg	Al	Si	P	S	Cl	Ar	K
1	2	3	4	5	6	7	8	9	10	11	12	13	14	15	16	17	18	19

number of electrons

very unreactive gases

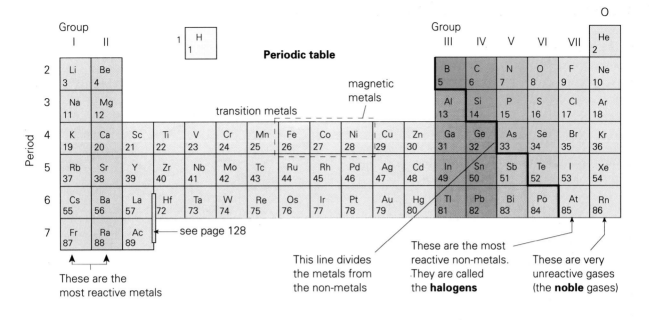

Periodic table

Group I, II, 1 H 1

2 Li 3, Be 4

3 Na 11, Mg 12

4 K 19, Ca 20, Sc 21, Ti 22, V 23, Cr 24, Mn 25, Fe 26, Co 27, Ni 28, Cu 29, Zn 30, Ga 31, Ge 32, As 33, Se 34, Br 35, Kr 36

5 Rb 37, Sr 38, Y 39, Zr 40, Nb 41, Mo 42, Tc 43, Ru 44, Rh 45, Pd 46, Ag 47, Cd 48, In 49, Sn 50, Sb 51, Te 52, I 53, Xe 54

6 Cs 55, Ba 56, La 57, Hf 72, Ta 73, W 74, Re 75, Os 76, Ir 77, Pt 78, Au 79, Hg 80, Tl 81, Pb 82, Bi 83, Po 84, At 85, Rn 86

7 Fr 87, Ra 88, Ac 89 — see page 128

Group III, IV, V, VI, VII, O; He 2; B 5, C 6, N 7, O 8, F 9, Ne 10; Al 13, Si 14, P 15, S 16, Cl 17, Ar 18

transition metals — magnetic metals

These are the most reactive metals

This line divides the metals from the non-metals

These are the most reactive non-metals. They are called the **halogens**

These are very unreactive gases (the **noble** gases)

Period

Some of the columns have *group* numbers. For example, the elements in Group I all have one electron in the outer shell and are reactive metals of low density. The elements in Group 0 all have full outer shells and are very unreactive gases.

Element	Symbol	Number of electrons				Total	
		Shell					
		1	2	3	4		
hydrogen	H	1				1	
helium	He	2				2	full shell
lithium	Li	2	1			3	
beryllium	Be	2	2			4	
boron	B	2	3			5	
carbon	C	2	4			6	
nitrogen	N	2	5			7	
oxygen	O	2	6			8	
fluorine	F	2	7			9	
neon	Ne	2	8			10	full shell
sodium	Na	2	8	1		11	
magnesium	Mg	2	8	2		12	
aluminium	Al	2	8	3		13	
silicon	Si	2	8	4		14	
phosphorus	P	2	8	5		15	
sulphur	S	2	8	6		16	
chlorine	Cl	2	8	7		17	
argon	Ar	2	8	8		18	full shell
potassium	K	2	8	8	1	19	

Electrons and reactions

Scientists think they can explain why elements in the same group have similar properties. It is because of their similar electron arrangements:

Electrons are the bits of atoms which take part in chemical reactions. For example, when sodium reacts with chlorine, a sodium atom's one outer electron is pulled across to fill the one space in a chlorine atom's outer shell. So, sodium and chlorine are both left with full outer shells. (See also Spread 3.8.)

A full outer shell is a very stable arrangement. Elements with full outer shells are very unreactive because the electrons tend to stay where they are. On the other hand, elements with one outer electron, or one unfilled space, are very reactive.

1 Give *three* features which are common to the elements in Group I.
2 Give *three* features which are common to the elements in Group 0.
3 How many outer-shell electrons do the elements have in a) Group II b) Group VI?
4 Use the periodic table to give as much information as you can about each of these elements: *krypton (Kr) caesium (Cs) cobalt (Co)*
5 Sodium has only one more electron than neon, yet its properties are very different. Why?

3·6 Moving particles

By the end of this spread, you should be able to:
* *describe the particles in a solid, liquid, and gas*
* *explain the links between particles, change of state, temperature, diffusion, and expansion*

Solids, liquids, and gases

Scientists have come up with an idea to explain how solids, liquids, and gases behave. They call this the *particle model of matter* :

Solids, liquids, and gases are made up of tiny particles. In water, for example, the particles are molecules. The particles are constantly on the move. They also attract each other. The attractions are strongest when the particles are close.

Water can be a solid, liquid or gas.

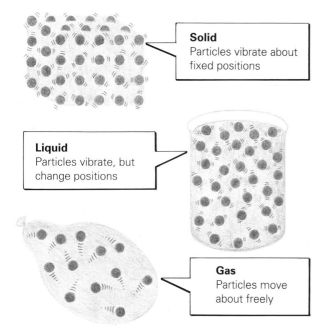

Solid
Particles vibrate about fixed positions

Liquid
Particles vibrate, but change positions

Gas
Particles move about freely

Solid The particles are held together by strong forces of attraction. The particles vibrate from side to side, but they cannot change positions.

Liquid The particles are still pulled together by forces of attraction. But strong vibrations mean that the particles have enough energy to change position and move past each other. So, the liquid can flow.

Gas The particles are spaced out, and almost free of any attractions. They move about at high speed, and quickly fill any space available.

Changing state

As something gets hotter its particles move faster.

If a very cold block of ice is heated, its particles vibrate faster. When their vibrations are strong enough, the particles can change position, so the solid becomes a liquid. In other words, the ice melts.

If water is heated, its particles vibrate faster. Some particles move fast enough to break free of the attractions holding them together. The liquid changes into a gas. In other words, the water becomes steam.

Even cold water can *evaporate* (change into gas). However, if water is hot enough, it produces bubbles of steam and evaporates rapidly. This is *boiling*.

Heat energy (see 4.7) is needed to change a solid into a liquid or a liquid into a gas. For example, if your hands are wet, they cool down as the evaporating water draws heat from them. The cooling effect of evaporation is used in the pipes of a refrigerator.

A change from solid to liquid, or liquid to gas, or back again, is called a change of *state*:

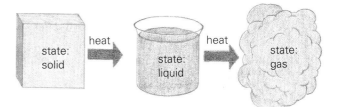

state: solid → heat → state: liquid → heat → state: gas

Temperature

When something gets hotter, and its particles move faster, scientists say that its **temperature** rises.

Everyday temperatures are normally measured on the **Celsius** scale (sometimes called the 'centigrade' scale.) Its unit of temperature is the **degree Celsius** (**ºC**). The numbers on this scale were specially chosen so that ice melts at 0 ºC and water boils at 100 ºC.

Wandering particles

Jostled by other particles around them, some particles wander about. That is why colours spread on top of a trifle. It also why smells spread. Smells are gas particles coming from food, or perfume, or anything smelly. The wandering of particles in this way is called **diffusion**.

Expansion

If a steel bar is heated, its particles vibrate more. As a result, they push each other a little further apart and the bar gets slightly bigger. In other words, the bar **expands**. **Expansion** affects other materials, not just steel. Expansion is usually too small to notice, but it can produce very strong forces. For example, gaps are left in bridges to allow for expansion on a hot day. Without a gap, the force of the expansion might crack the structure.

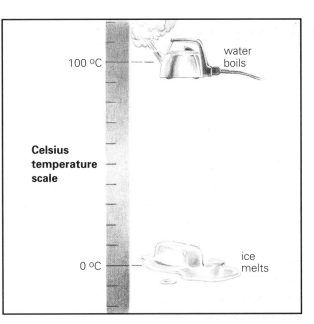

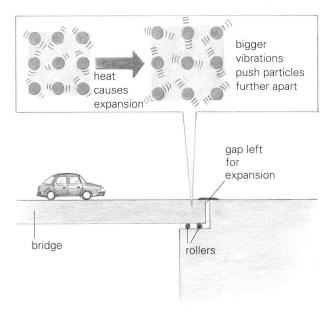

Diffusion on top of a trifle

1 Comparing their behaviour, what differences are there between the particles in
   a) a solid and a liquid b) a liquid and a gas?
2 What happens to the particles in something if the temperature rises?
3 On the Celsius scale, what is the temperature of a) melting ice b) boiling water?
4 How do smells spread? What is the process called?
5 Why does a bar of steel expand when it is heated?
6 Why is it important to leave plenty of slack when overhead wires are put up on a hot day?

Gases, laws, and particles

By the end of this spread, you should be able to:
- *describe and use the gas laws*
- *describe how the particle model helps explain the gas laws*

Gases are squashy. So a gas does not necessarily expand when heated. If the container can resist the expansion, the volume will not change. However, there will be more **pressure** on the container. When dealing with gases, there are always *three* factors to consider: pressure, volume, and temperature.

Gas pressure

In a gas, the particles move around at high speed. As they collide with the sides of the container, they produce a force. This is the force which keeps balloons and tyres inflated. The more concentrated the force, the greater the pressure. (For more on pressure and its meaning, see spread 4.11.)

Pressure can be measured using a unit called the **pascal (Pa)**. However, a larger unit, the **kilopascal (kPa)** is often more convenient. 1 kPa = 1000 Pa.

The gas laws

Scientists have carried out many experiments with gases in containers. There are some typical results on the opposite page. In each of the experiments shown, one of the factors pressure *(P)*, volume *(V)*, or temperature *(T)* has been kept fixed, while the other two have been varied.

The results show that there are laws linking the pressure, volume, and temperature of a trapped gas. But the temperature *must* be measured using the **Kelvin scale** rather than the Celsius scale. There is some information about the Kelvin scale on the right.

The results can be combined in a single gas law. The law is especially useful if the pressure, volume, and temperature all change at the same time:

If conditions for a fixed mass of gas change so that P_1, V_1, and T_1 become P_2, V_2, and T_2, then:

$$\frac{P_1 \times V_1}{T_1} = \frac{P_2 \times V_2}{T_2}$$

In a balloon, P, V, and T can all change.

The Kelvin temperature scale

According to the results on the opposite page, if you keep on cooling a gas, its volume eventually falls to zero. This is because the particles get slower and slower until they stop hitting the sides of the container and causing a pressure. The temperature at which this happens is −273 °C. It is called **absolute zero**. It is the lowest possible temperature because the particles cannot go any slower.

The Kelvin temperature scale uses absolute zero as its zero. Its 'degree', is the **kelvin (K)**. This chart shows the link between Kelvin and Celsius temperatures:

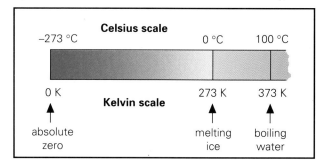

How *P* changes with *T*	How *V* changes with *T*	How *P* changes with *V*
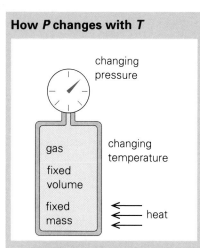	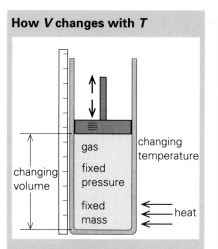	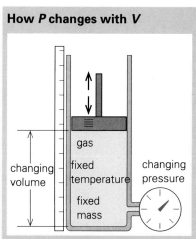

How *P* changes with *T*

Typical results:

Temperature in K	200	400	600	800
Pressure in kPa	100	200	300	400

From these results:
- *P* doubles if *T* doubles.... and so on
- *P/T* has the same value each time: in this case, 0.5.

Put another way:

For a fixed mass of gas, P is proportional to T, provided V is fixed.

This is called the ***pressure law***.

How *V* changes with *T*

Typical results:

Temperature in K	200	400	600	800
Volume in cm³	150	300	450	600

From these results:
- *V* doubles if *T* doubles.... and so on
- *V/T* has the same value each time: in this case, 0.75.

Put another way:

For a fixed mass of gas, V is proportional to T, provided P is fixed.

This is called the ***volume law***.

How *P* changes with *V*

Typical results:

Volume in cm³	50	40	25	20
Pressure in kPa	200	250	400	500

From these results:
- *P* doubles if *V* halves.... and so on
- *P* x *V* has the same value each time: in this case, 10 000.

Put another way:

For a fixed mass of gas, P is proportional 1/V, provided T is fixed.

This is called ***Boyle's law***.

Explaining the laws

Here are some examples of how the particle model can help explain the gas laws:

Temperature rises, volume fixed
The particles move faster. They collide with the sides of the container at a higher speed, so the ***pressure rises***.

Temperature rises, pressure fixed
The gas is free to expand. The particles move faster, but are more spaced out. The ***volume rises***.

Volume rises, temperature fixed
The particles keep the same speed. However, they are more spaced out, so the collisons with the sides of the container are less concentrated. The ***pressure falls***.

1 Change these temperatures into kelvin:
   a) 0 °C b) 100 °C c) 27 °C d) -73 °C
2 Use the results above to plot a graph of
   a) *P* against *T* b) *V* against *T* c) *P* against *V*
   d) *P* against 1/*V*. Before you do the last one, you will have to work out values of 1/*V* on a calculator. When you have plotted the graphs, describe in words what each one shows.
3 Using ideas about particles, explain why the pressure rises if a) you squash a balloon b) a gas canister is left too close to a fire.
4 A balloon contains 6 m³ of helium. As it rises through the atmosphere, the pressure falls from 100 kPa to 50 kPa, but the temperature stays the same. What is the new volume of the balloon?

Atoms and bonds

By the end of this spread, you should be able to:
- describe the particles in an atom
- explain how atoms stick together to form compounds

Inside atoms

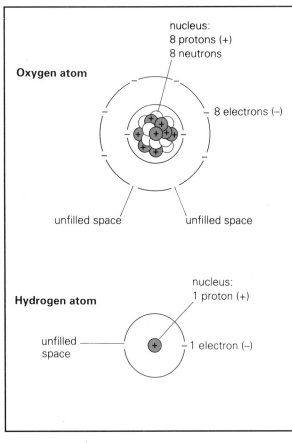

Inside molecules

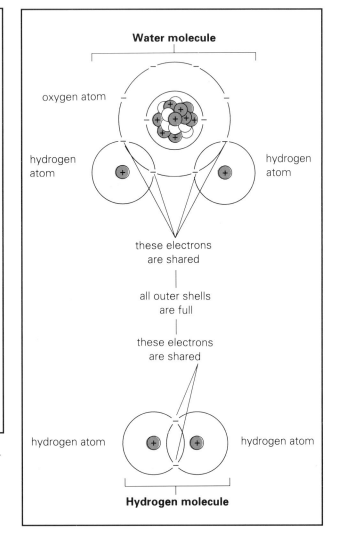

In an atom, **electrons** move around a central **nucleus**. The nucleus is itself made up of smaller particles called **protons** and **neutrons** (apart from hydrogen, which just has one proton as its nucleus).

Protons and electrons have an **electric charge**. Protons have a **positive (+)** charge. Electrons have an equal **negative (–)** charge. Neutrons are uncharged.

Atoms have the same number of electrons (–) as protons (+), so, overall, they are uncharged.

Opposite charges (+ and –) attract each other with an electric force (see also Spread 4.1). That is why electrons stay around the nucleus. Protons repel each other, but this 'pushing apart' is overcome by another force which binds the nucleus together.

Some atoms stick together in clumps called **molecules**. They do so by sharing electrons. They are held together by electric forces called **bonds**.

In a water molecule, the two hydrogen atoms share their electrons with the oxygen atom. In this way, the atoms all end up with full outer shells. Bonding by sharing electrons is called **covalent bonding.**

Some molecules have atoms of the same type. For example each molecule of hydrogen gas is made up of two hydrogen atoms.

Forces between molecules

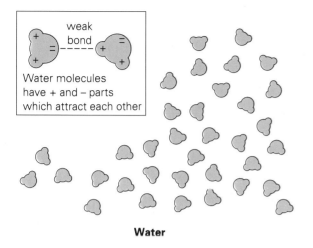

Water

Dissolving

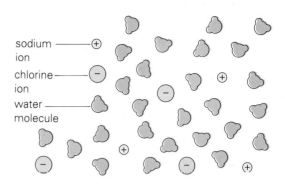

Sodium chloride dissolved in water

Bonds hold atoms together in a molecule. Much weaker bonds pull some molecules together to form solids and liquids. For example:

In a water molecule, the bonding electrons are not equally shared between the atoms. This means that the oxygen is slightly negative (–) and the hydrogen slightly positive (+). Positive (+) parts of one molecule are attracted to negative (–) parts on others, so water molecules tend to stick to each other. However this weak bond is easily broken by heating. That is why ice melts so easily.

Ions

Some atoms stick together because electrons are transferred from one to another. For example:

In sodium chloride (common salt), each sodium atom has *lost* an electron, making it positively (+) charged. Each chlorine atom has *gained* an electron, making it negatively (–) charged. The opposite charges attract, holding the charged atoms tightly together in a lattice. The result is a crystal of sodium chloride.

Charged atoms are called ***ions***. So sodium chloride is made up of positive (+) sodium ions and negative (–) chlorine ions. This type of bonding is called ***ionic bonding***.

The bonds between ions are much stronger than those between molecules. That is why ionic compounds, such as sodium chloride, have higher melting temperatures than covalent compounds, such as water. The particles are more difficult to separate.

Ionic compounds, such as sodium chloride, dissolve in water. When sodium chloride dissolves, it splits into sodium ions (+) and chlorine ions (–), which spread between the water molecules. Water with ions in it will conduct electricity (see spread 4.1).

---

1. Which particles in an atom have a) positive charge b) negative charge c) no charge?
2. A boron atom has 5 protons and 6 neutrons. How many electrons does it have?
3. What are *ions*?
4. What holds the atoms together in a water molecule?
5. Why does ice melt at a lower temperature than sodium chloride?
6. Describe what happens to its particles when sodium chloride dissolves in water.

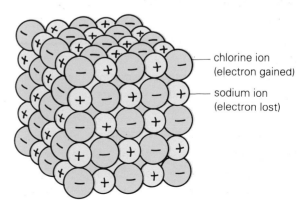

Crystal of sodium chloride

Radioactivity

By the end of this spread, you should be able to:
• explain why some substances are radioactive
• describe the three main types of nuclear radiation and their effects

Isotopes

Atoms of the same element are not all alike. Elements can exist in different versions, with different numbers of neutrons in the nucleus. These different versions are called **isotopes**. For example:

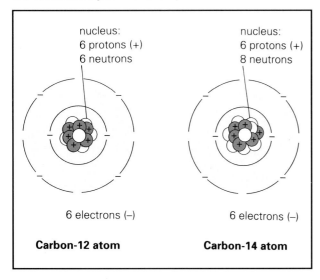

nucleus:
6 protons (+)
6 neutrons

nucleus:
6 protons (+)
8 neutrons

6 electrons (−)

6 electrons (−)

Carbon-12 atom

Carbon-14 atom

Most carbon atoms have 6 protons and 6 neutrons in the nucleus. This common isotope is called carbon-12 (12 is the total of protons plus neutrons). But some carbon atoms have 6 protons and 8 neutrons. This rare isotope is carbon-14.

Nuclear radiation

Some isotopes have unstable atoms. In time, the nucleus breaks up, and shoots out a tiny particle, or burst of wave energy, or both. This 'radiates' from the nucleus. It is called **nuclear radiation**. If a substance gives out nuclear radiation, scientists say that it is **radioactive**.

Some of the materials in nuclear power stations are highly radioactive. But nuclear radiation comes from many natural sources as well, as shown in the table on the right. This means that there is a small amount of nuclear radiation around us all the time. Scientists call it **background radiation**.

Containers for radioactive waste must be strong enough to withstand crashes like this.

Ionizing effect

Nuclear radiation can remove electrons from atoms in its path. In other words it can make ions: it has an **ionizing** effect. Ionizing radiation can be very dangerous. It may stop cells in vital organs working properly. It can also damage the chemical instructions in normal cells so that the cells grow abnormally and cause cancer. However, in **radiotherapy** treatment, carefully-directed radiation (gamma rays) is used to kill cancer cells.

Isotopes		
Stable	*Unstable, radioactive*	*Found in...*
carbon-12 carbon-13	carbon-14	air, plants, animals
potassium-39 potassium-41	potassium-40	rocks, plants, sea-water
	uranium-234 uranium-235 uranium-238	rocks

Alpha, beta, and gamma

There are three main types of nuclear radiation: **alpha** particles, **beta** particles, and **gamma** rays. They can be detected by a **Geiger-Müller tube (GM tube)**, connected to an electronic counter or meter.

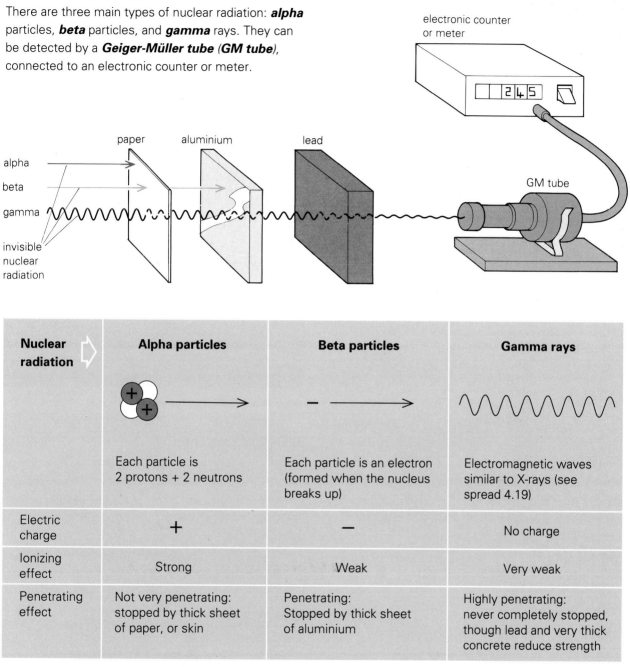

Nuclear radiation	Alpha particles	Beta particles	Gamma rays
	Each particle is 2 protons + 2 neutrons	Each particle is an electron (formed when the nucleus breaks up)	Electromagnetic waves similar to X-rays (see spread 4.19)
Electric charge	+	−	No charge
Ionizing effect	Strong	Weak	Very weak
Penetrating effect	Not very penetrating: stopped by thick sheet of paper, or skin	Penetrating: Stopped by thick sheet of aluminium	Highly penetrating: never completely stopped, though lead and very thick concrete reduce strength

1 Comparing atoms of *carbon-12* and *carbon-14*:
   a) What do the numbers '12' and '14' tell you?
   b) In what ways are the atoms the same?
   c) How are the atoms different?
2 If a substance is *radioactive*, what does this mean?
3 Nuclear radiation has an *ionizing effect*. What does this mean?

4 Why can ionizing radiation be dangerous?
5 What are the three main types of nuclear radiation?
6 Which type of radiation is stopped by skin or thick paper?
7 Which type of radiation can penetrate lead?
8 Which type of radiation is most ionizing?
9 Explain what is meant by *background radiation*.

Chemical reactions

By the end of this spread, you should be able to:
- *give the evidence for a chemical change*
- *describe different types of chemical reaction*
- *describe factors affecting the rate of a reaction*

When iron and sulphur join, they make a completely new substance, iron sulphide. This is an example of a **chemical change**. A **chemical reaction** has taken place between the iron and the sulphur. Iron sulphide is the **product**. The reaction can be described using this **word equation**:

iron + sulphur → iron sulphide

Signs of chemical change

If a chemical change has taken place:

One or more new substances are formed
In the reaction above, iron is a metal, sulphur is a yellow powder, but iron sulphide is a black solid.

Energy is given out or taken in
When iron reacts with sulphur, heat is given out. Reactions which give out heat are called **exothermic** reactions. On the other hand, some reactions take in heat. They are **endothermic**.

The change is usually difficult to reverse
Several reactions are needed to change iron sulphide back into iron and sulphur.

Very rapid chemical reactions

Speed of reaction

Before substances can react, their moving particles (atoms, ions, or molecules) must meet. The speed of a reaction depends on how quickly this happens. Below are some of the factors it depends on:

Size of bits A powdered substance reacts more quickly than one with larger bits. This is because the powder has a much bigger surface area, so more reacting particles come into contact.

Temperature A reaction goes faster if the temperature rises. This is because the reacting particles collide with each other more quickly.

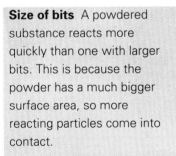

Catalyst This is any chemical added which makes a reaction go faster without being used up itself. It helps other particles meet and join more quickly.

Concentration Increasing the concentration of a substance makes a reaction go faster. A higher concentration means that more particles are likely to meet and join.

Types of chemical reaction

Here are some different types of chemical reaction:

Synthesis (combination) Two substances join to make a single new substance. For example, this reaction takes place when magnesium burns:

magnesium + oxygen → magnesium oxide
(metal)　　　(gas)　　　　　(grey ash)

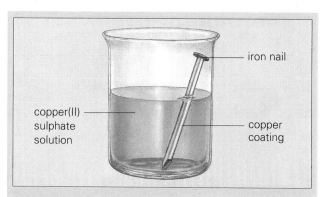

iron nail

copper(II) sulphate solution

copper coating

Displacement One substance pushes out another and takes its place. For example, if an iron nail is placed in copper(II) sulphate solution, some iron dissolves and displaces copper in the solution. The copper is deposited on the nail as a brown coating:

iron + copper sulphate → copper + iron sulphate

There is a displacement reaction whenever a metal reacts with an acid. The metal displaces hydrogen in the solution. (Remember: all acids contain hydrogen).

Acid-base If an acid reacts with a base, it can form a neutral solution containing a salt. (See Spread 3.4.)

Redox When hydrogen gas is passed over hot copper(II) oxide, this reaction takes place (Symbols have also been used so that you can see what is happening to the atoms):

copper(II) oxide + hydrogen → copper + water
　　CuO　　　+　H_2　→　Cu　+　H_2O

This is an example of a redox reaction:
Copper(II) oxide has *lost* oxygen: it has been **reduced**.
Hydrogen has *gained* oxygen: it has been **oxidized**.
Reduction and **ox**idation always happen together, which is why the name **redox** is used.

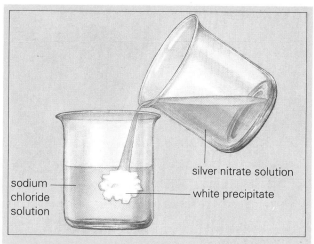

silver nitrate solution

sodium chloride solution

white precipitate

Precipitation When some solutions are mixed, they react and give a product which is insoluble (it doesn't dissolve). It appears as tiny, solid bits called a ***precipitate***. For example:

silver nitrate	+	sodium chloride	→	silver chloride	+	sodium nitrate
(soluble)		(soluble)		(insoluble precipitate)		(soluble)

Decomposition A substance splits to form simpler substances. For example, if calcium carbonate is heated to 1100 °C, it splits to form calcium oxide and carbon dioxide:

heat
calcium carbonate → calcium oxide + carbon dioxide
　(limestone)　　　　　(quicklime)　　　　　(gas)

1 Solid ice melts to become liquid water. Explain why this is not a chemical change.
2 Magnesium burning is a chemical reaction.
   a) What is the product of this reaction?
   b) Is the reaction *exothermic* or *endothermic*? Explain your answer.
3 Which would burn most quickly, a strip of magnesium or powdered magesium? Why?
4 Warm, liquid glucose, with yeast added as a catalyst, splits up to form two simpler substances: ethanol and carbon dioxide.
   a) What type of reaction is this?
   b) What is a *catalyst*?
   c) Write a word equation for the reaction.

Burning and oxides

By the end of this spread, you should be able to:
- describe the products of burning
- explain what conditions are needed for burning
- explain what causes corrosion and food oxidation

Combustion

Combustion is another word for burning. It happens when substances react with oxygen in the air, and gives out energy as heat and light.

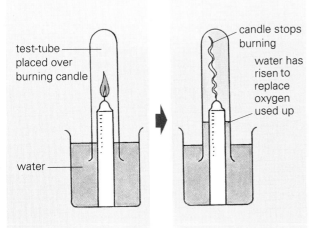

test-tube placed over burning candle

candle stops burning

water has risen to replace oxygen used up

water

This experiment shows that about 1/5 of the air is used up when something burns. That is because about 1/5 of the air is oxygen.

When an element burns, it becomes *oxidized*. The product of the reaction is an *oxide*. For example:

sulphur + oxygen → sulphur dioxide

magnesium + oxygen → magnesium oxide

Extra weight If you burn magnesium ribbon in a crucible and trap the ash, the ash weighs more than the magnesium because of the added oxygen:

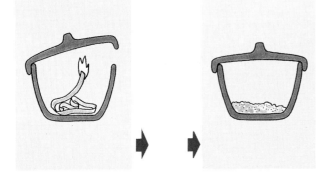

Burning fuels

Fuels include wood, coal, petrol, and natural gas (methane). Most are compounds of hydrogen and carbon. When they burn, the main products are carbon dioxide and water. For example:

methane + oxygen → carbon dioxide + water

| atoms of C and H | atoms of O | atoms of C and O | atoms of H and O |

Some fuels are compounds of hydrogen, carbon, and oxygen. Ethanol (alcohol) is an example. Fuels like this also produce carbon dioxide and water when they burn.

Respiration is a kind of 'slow combustion' without any flames (see Spread 2.2). Our body cells use it to get energy from glucose (a compound of carbon, hydrogen, and oxygen):

glucose + oxygen → carbon dioxide + water

> **Testing for carbon dioxide** Carbon dioxide turns a liquid called *lime water* milky. You can use this fact to tell that there is carbon dioxide in the air you breathe out. Just gently blow through lime water with a drinking straw and watch what happens.

Testing for oxygen Fuels which burn in air burn more fiercely in pure oxygen. You can use this fact to test for oxygen. If a smouldering wooden splint is put into a jar containing oxygen, the splint will burst into flames.

Fire!

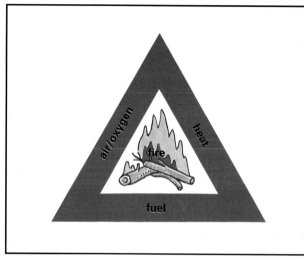

This **combustion triangle** shows the three things needed for burning. Removing any of them stops the burning. So firefighters have three ways of putting out a fire:

- **Cutting off the fuel**, for example by turning off gas at the mains.
- **Cutting off the air supply** by using fire blankets, foam, or carbon dioxide gas.
- **Getting rid of the heat**, for example, by cooling things down with water.

Note: water is not safe for some fires. It conducts electricity and can give people shocks. And it can make burning fat or oil splatter and spread.

Foods oxidizing

Things do not necessarily have to burn to react with oxygen. For example:

Some foods react with oxygen in the air. Fats such as butter and lard are like this. When they become oxidized, they taste very unpleasant. People say they are **rancid**. Keeping fats in a refrigerator slows the oxidizing process. Keeping out the air is another way of tackling the problem. For example, crisp manufacturers fill crisp bags with nitrogen to stop the fat on the crisps becoming oxidized.

Corrosion

If a metal is reactive, its surface may be attacked by air, water, or other substances around it. The effect is called **corrosion**. For example, when iron corrodes, the iron becomes oxidized, and the product is the brown, flaky substance we call **rust**. Steel, which is mainly iron, can also go rusty.

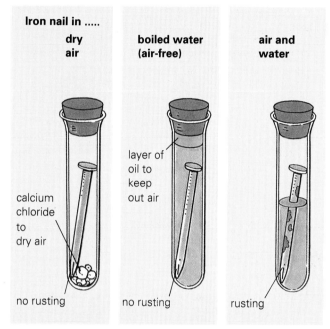

This experiment shows that air *and* water are needed for rusting. Dry air alone has no effect. Nor does water alone (if all air has been removed by boiling).

To stop iron and steel rusting, they can be coated with paint, grease, plastic, or a thin layer of non-corroding metal such as tin. This keeps out the air and water. (Stainless steel does not rust, but is far too expensive for many jobs.)

1 What *three* things are necessary for burning?
2 What is the product when an element (such as sulphur) burns?
3 What are the products when a fuel (such as methane) burns?
4 How could you tell whether a gas was a) carbon dioxide b) oxygen?
5 *Two* things are needed for iron or steel to rust. What are they?
6 What problems are caused by food oxidation? Describe *two* ways in which these can be prevented.

Getting at metals

By the end of this spread, you should be able to:
- explain why different methods are needed to extract metals from their ores
- explain how iron, steel, pure copper, and aluminium are produced

Most of our metals come from rocks in the ground. A few occur naturally as elements. But most are in compounds called **ores**. Bonds which form easily are also the most difficult to break. So the more reactive a metal is, the more difficult it is to separate from its ore. (See the table on the opposite page and the information on the **reactivity series** in Spread 3.2.)

Gold is very unreactive

Iron and steel

Haematite (iron ore) is a compound of iron and oxygen. The iron can be extracted by a process called **smelting** which takes place in a **blast furnace**. Very hot limestone and coke are used to remove oxygen from the ore so that molten (melted) iron is left.

Iron from a blast furnace is called **pig iron**. It is not pure, and has a carbon content of about 4%. This makes it hard, but brittle.

To make steel, oxygen is passed through molten pig iron to 'burn off' most of the impurities, including carbon. Then controlled amounts of carbon (and other elements) are put back in. The result is the tough, springy alloy we call steel. Its carbon content is usually less than 1.5%.

Blast furnace

1 Iron ore, coke, and limestone loaded through here

5 Waste gases leave here

400 °C

4 Reaction between carbon monoxide and iron ore produces molten iron, which trickles down

iron ore, limestone, and coke

3 Reactions between coke (carbon) and limestone (calcium carbonate) produce carbon monoxide

1800 °C

2 Hot air blasted through here

6 Slag (waste) from other reactions collects here

7 Molten iron collects here

---

1 In a blast furnace, why are the coke and limestone needed?
2 What method must be used to separate the most reactive metals from their ores?
3 During the electrolysis of copper sulphate, why does pure copper collect on the cathode?

4 How is pig iron made into steel?
5 *Gold   copper   aluminium*
   a) Which of these metals is the most reactive?
   b) Which is only found as an element? Why?
   c) Which is the most difficult to separate from its ore? Why?

Metal	Ore/how found	Reactivity of metal	Separating metal from ore
potassium (K) sodium (Na) calcium (Ca) magnesium (Mg) aluminium (Al)	silvine (KCl) rock salt (NaCl) limestone ($CaCO_3$) magnesite ($MgCO_3$) bauxite (Al_2O_3)	very reactive	electrolysis (using electricity)
zinc (Zn) iron (Fe) tin (Sn) lead (Pb)	calamine ($ZnCO_3$) haematite (Fe_2O_3) cassiterite (SnO_2) galena (PbS)	getting more difficult to separate from ore	heating with carbon or carbon monoxide
copper (Cu) silver (Ag)	chalcopyrite ($CuFeS_2$) and as an element argentite (Ag_2S) and as an element		heating in air
gold (Au)	as an element	unreactive	

Electrolysis and copper

Electricity can be used to decompose (split) a compound. The process is called **electrolysis**.

Impure copper can be purified by electrolysis. The diagram on the right shows how. The liquid in the tank is copper(II) sulphate solution. This is the **electrolyte**. Dipping into it are two metal **electrodes**: the **cathode** (connected to the – terminal of the battery) and the **anode** (connected to the + terminal). The lump of impure copper is the anode.

In the tank, copper(II) sulphate splits to form positive (+) copper ions and negative (–) sulphate ions. The copper ions (+) are attracted to the cathode (–), where they build up as a layer of pure copper. As this happens, copper from the impure lump dissolves in the electrolyte to replace the copper ions. In this way, copper is removed from the impure lump and pure copper collects on the cathode.

Aluminium

Aluminium can be separated from its ore (bauxite) by electrolysis. The electrolyte is hot, purified bauxite (aluminium oxide) dissolved in a molten aluminium compound called cryolite. The aluminium oxide splits into positive (+) aluminium ions and negative (–) oxide ions. The aluminium ions (+) are attracted to the cathode (–), where they become aluminium atoms. These collect at the bottom of the tank as molten aluminium.

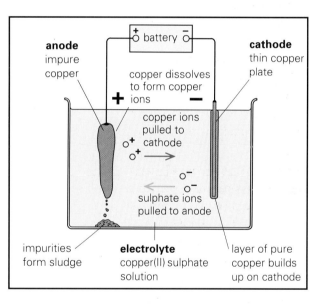

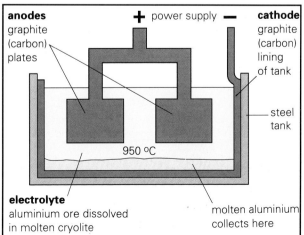

From water and rocks

By the end of this spread, you should be able to:
- *explain why salt, water, and limestone are useful, and how new materials can be made from them*

On Earth, there are many natural materials which can be processed to make other things. These are called **raw materials**. They include salt, water, and rocks.

Common salt

Common salt (sodium chloride) is very plentiful on Earth. Sea-water has salt dissolved in it (about 3%). Solid salt is also found underground, as on the right. In this form, it is known as rock salt.

Salt has many uses, and is the raw material for making many other chemicals:

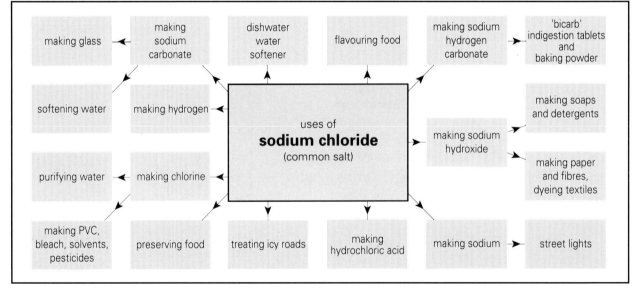

- making glass
- making sodium carbonate
- dishwater water softener
- flavouring food
- making sodium hydrogen carbonate
- 'bicarb' indigestion tablets and baking powder
- softening water
- making hydrogen
- making soaps and detergents
- purifying water
- making chlorine
- **uses of sodium chloride (common salt)**
- making sodium hydroxide
- making paper and fibres, dyeing textiles
- making PVC, bleach, solvents, pesticides
- preserving food
- treating icy roads
- making hydrochloric acid
- making sodium
- street lights

More from electrolysis

When sodium chloride dissolves in water, its ions are free to move. So it can be electrolysed. The diagram on the right shows what happens when this is done using graphite (carbon) electrodes:

Hydrogen gas bubbles off at the cathode (the hydrogen comes from the water).

Chlorine gas bubbles off at the anode (the chlorine comes from the salt). The electrolyte also contains sodium ions and hydroxide ions. In an industrial version of the process on the right, these form sodium hydroxide which can be collected.

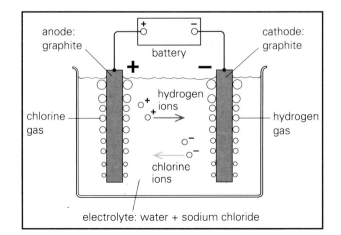

anode: graphite | battery | cathode: graphite

chlorine gas | hydrogen ions | hydrogen gas

chlorine ions

electrolyte: water + sodium chloride

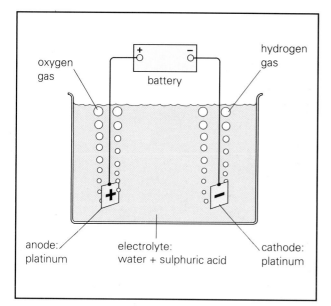

The diagram above shows the electrolysis of acidified water (water with acid in it). Platinum electrodes are being used. This time, the effect is to split the water into hydrogen gas and oxygen gas:

$$water \xrightarrow[\text{electricity}]{\text{acid}} hydrogen + oxygen$$

Limestone

Limestone is one of the most common rocks in Britain. It is mainly calcium carbonate, and was formed from the shells and bones of sea creatures which lived millions of years ago.

The building industry uses huge amounts of limestone:

Cement is made from limestone. It is produced by burning limestone, clay, and sand in a kiln, and then grinding the product with gypsum.

Chippings are often tiny pieces of limestone. Mixed with tar, they make Tarmac for roads. They are also used in blast furnaces and in making concrete.

Concrete is made by mixing chippings, sand, cement, and water, and leaving them to set.

Microbes at work

Some new materials are made by **microbes** (microscopic organisms). For example, alcohol is made by microbes during **fermentation**. For more details, see Spread 2.11.

Kettles, kidneys, and caves

Rainwater is slightly acid. It slowly reacts with limestone (calcium carbonate) to form calcium hydrogencarbonate, which dissolves in water. In limestone areas, the tap water contains dissolved calcium hydrogencarbonate. This makes it more difficult for soap to lather. People say that the water is **hard**.

When water is boiled, dissolved calcium hydrogen-carbonate changes back to solid calcium carbonate. This is the **scale** which builds up on the insides of kettles and water pipes.

In people's kidneys, calcium carbonate can form very attractive but painful crystals called **kidney stones**. In dripping, limestone caves, calcium carbonate forms **stalactites** and **stalagmites**.

---

1. Look at the chart on the opposite page, showing some uses of common salt:
   a) Give *three* direct uses of salt
   b) Give *three* substances made in chemical reactions which use salt.
2. If sodium chloride solution is electrolysed using graphite electrodes, hydrogen gas is produced.
   a) Where does the hydrogen come from?
   b) What other gas is produced?
   c) What is this other gas used for?
3. Give *two* reasons why limestone is important for the building industry.

From oil and air

By the end of this spread, you should be able to:
• describe some of the substances in oil and air, and how these can be obtained and used

Oil and air are mixtures. They contain useful substances which can be turned into new materials by chemical reactions. For example, sustances in oil are used to make plastics like those on the right.

Oil

Oil companies get their oil from the ground. They call it **crude oil**. It was formed from the remains of tiny sea animals and plants which died millions of years ago. It is a mixture of substances called **hydrocarbons**. These are compounds of hydrogen and carbon.

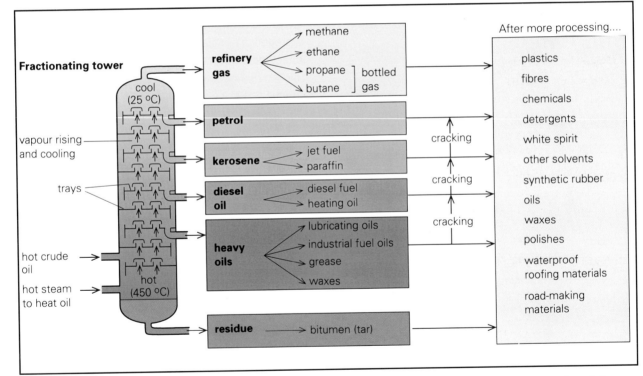

At an **oil refinery**, the different substances in crude oil are separated in a **fractionating tower**. The oil is boiled so that most rises up the tower as vapour (gas). As it rises, it cools. Different substances condense (turn liquid) at different temperatures, and are collected at different levels. The different parts of the mixture are called **fractions**. Separating fractions by boiling is called **fractional distillation**.

Heavier fractions have longer molecules than lighter fractions. Using a chemical process called **cracking**, long molecules can be broken up to make shorter ones. So, if there is too much diesel oil, it can be changed into petrol by cracking.

Short molecules can also be joined together to make longer one. This process is called **polymerization**. Plastics are made by polymerization.

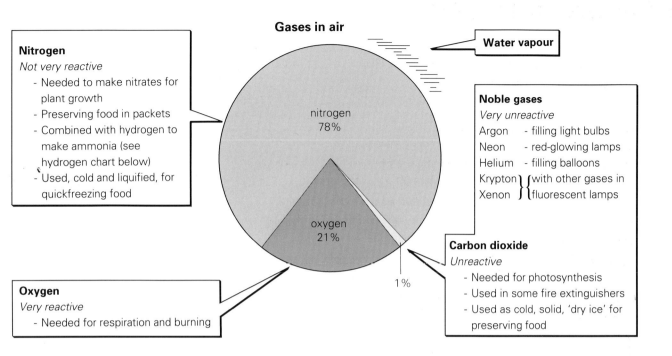

Gases in air

Nitrogen
Not very reactive
- Needed to make nitrates for plant growth
- Preserving food in packets
- Combined with hydrogen to make ammonia (see hydrogen chart below)
- Used, cold and liquified, for quickfreezing food

nitrogen
78%

oxygen
21%

1%

Water vapour

Noble gases
Very unreactive
Argon   - filling light bulbs
Neon   - red-glowing lamps
Helium   - filling balloons
Krypton ⎫ ⎧ with other gases in
Xenon   ⎭ ⎩ fluorescent lamps

Oxygen
Very reactive
- Needed for respiration and burning

Carbon dioxide
Unreactive
- Needed for photosynthesis
- Used in some fire extinguishers
- Used as cold, solid, 'dry ice' for preserving food

Natural gas, and hydrogen

Many heating systems and cookers use natural gas as their fuel. Natural gas was formed in a similar way to oil. Like oil, it is collected from underground. It is mainly methane, and is similar to the gas collected at the top of an oil fractionating tower.

Methane (CH_4) is industry's main source of hydrogen. The hydrogen is produced when a mixture of methane and steam is passed over catalysts. The chart below shows some of the uses of hydrogen:

Air

Air is a mixture of gases (see chart above). They are separated as follows:

First, the carbon dioxide and water vapour are removed. Next, the remaining air is cooled to −200 °C, so that it turns liquid (apart from neon and helium, which are removed). Then the liquid air is slowly warmed up. The gases boil off at different temperatures and are collected separately. This is another example of **fractional distillation**.

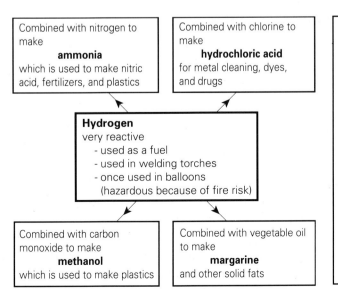

Combined with nitrogen to make
ammonia
which is used to make nitric acid, fertilizers, and plastics

Combined with chlorine to make
hydrochloric acid
for metal cleaning, dyes, and drugs

Hydrogen
very reactive
- used as a fuel
- used in welding torches
- once used in balloons (hazardous because of fire risk)

Combined with carbon monoxide to make
methanol
which is used to make plastics

Combined with vegetable oil to make
margarine
and other solid fats

1 Why are the substances in crude oil called *hydrocarbons*?
2 Name *three* fuels extracted from crude oil.
3 What is *cracking*? Why is it done?
4 Which is the most plentiful gas in air? Give *two* uses of this gas.
5 In this spread (3.14) and the one before (3.13), there are *three* different ways of producing hydrogen. What are they?
6 Name *two* gases which will make balloons float. Which is the safer? Why?
7 Look at the methods used for separating the substances in oil and in air. In what ways are the two methods similar?

3.15 Weather

By the end of this spread, you should be able to:
- *explain how the weather can change, and why*
- *interpret weather maps*
- *describe some of the effects of weathering*

We live at the bottom of an ocean of air called the atmosphere. It is more than 100 km deep, but most of the air lies within 10 km of the Earth's surface. Changes in this air give us our weather.

At sea level, air pressure is about **100 000 pascals (Pa)**. On many weather maps, this would be marked as **1000 millibars (mb)**. It is equivalent to the weight of ten cars pressing on every metre squared! (For more on pressure, see spreads 3.7 and 4.11).

Winds Air pressure varies slightly from one region to another. Air tends to flow from high pressure to low pressure. This causes winds.
Temperature differences also cause winds. Some places have more sunshine than others. Also, the land tends to warm up more quickly than the sea. As warm air rises, cooler air flows in to take its place. This is an example of **convection** (see Spread 4.8)

Clouds Water on the Earth's surface evaporates: it turns into a gas called water vapour. This happens most quickly when the air is warm and dry.
When water vapour cools, it condenses (changes to liquid). In the air, it turns into billions of tiny water droplets called **clouds**. Fog and **mist** are really the same as clouds. In some clouds, the droplets are frozen as ice crystals.

Dew and frost
Water vapour condenses on cold ground or plants to form **dew**. Frozen dew is called **frost**.

Thunder and lightning
Air movements and a temperature difference can make electric charge build up in a cloud. A sudden flow of charge lights up the air as **lightning**. It heats up the air as well. The rapid expansion produces a noise called **thunder**.

Rain, snow, and hail If the tiny water droplets in a cloud stick together into larger drops, they may fall as **rain**. If it is cold, they may form larger ice crystals and fall as **snow**. Sometimes, tiny droplets freeze, and gather extra layers of ice as they are carried up and down by air currents in a cloud. Then they fall as **hail**. Rain, snow, and hail are all called **precipitation**, which means 'something falling'.

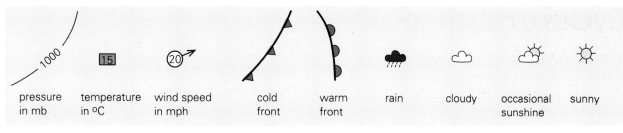

pressure in mb	temperature in °C	wind speed in mph	cold front	warm front	rain	cloudy	occasional sunshine	sunny
1000	15	20						

Here is a weather map:

Britain is in an area of low pressure, called a **depression**. This is centred north of Ireland.

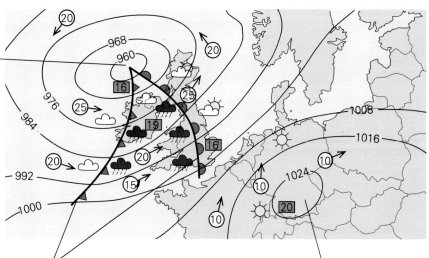

Over most of Britain, the winds are blowing in from the south-west. They have been travelling over the sea, so they are carrying plenty of water vapour which will eventually fall as rain. Hilly areas will tend to get most rain because the hills make the moving air rise and cool.

Between these **fronts**, there is a 'tongue' of warm, damp air with colder, drier air pushing in on either side. Rainclouds are forming near the fronts because the warm, damp air is being pushed up and cooled. This is where most rain will fall.

Over Germany, there is an area of high pressure called an **anticyclone**. Winds are blowing out from this area. The air is dry because it has not been travelling over water. No clouds are forming, so the anticyclone is bringing fine weather.

Weathering

The surfaces of rocks, soil, and stonework can be damaged by the weather. This is called **weathering**. For example, frost will crack pieces from rock (because water expands when it freezes). And rain, which is slightly acid, will eat into stonework.

1 What are clouds? How are they formed?
2 What causes frost? How can frost cause damage?
3 Look at the map above. How can you tell that there is a low pressure area north of Ireland?
4 Why is most rain falling near the two fronts?
5 In Britain, why do winds from the south-west tend to bring rain?
6 Why do hilly areas tend to get most rain?
7 What type of weather does an anticyclone (high pressure area) usually bring? Why?

The effects of weathering

Cycles of change

By the end of this spread, you should be able to:
* *explain how water is used over and over again*
* *describe some of the problems caused by providing a water supply*
* *explain how materials from rocks are used over and over again*

The water cycle

In one way or another, all our water comes from the sea:

Supply problems

There are many problems in supplying tap-water:
* Building reservoirs changes the landscape and affects wildlife.
* Taking too much water from undergound can change conditions on the surface. For example, it can dry out the habitats of some wildlife.
* If sewage or chemical waste is not disposed of carefully, it can contaminate the water supply.

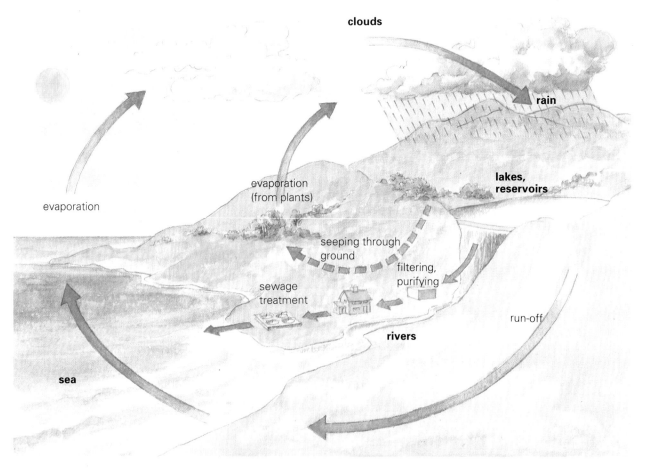

The Sun heats the sea, and water evaporates to become vapour. The vapour rises and condenses to forms clouds. These release their water as rain, often when they are blown over high ground. Rain seeps into the ground, runs into streams and rivers, and flows back into the sea. Also, plants take water from the soil and put some if back into the air as vapour. In this way, water is always being recycled. This is called the **water cycle**.

Humans also take part in the water cycle. We build reservoirs to trap water for our houses and factories. Our waste water and sewage is put back into the sea, though it is sometimes purified first.

Some water takes many thousands of years to complete the cycle. It collects in huge areas of underground, porous ('holey') rock called **aquifers**. These too are used as a source of tap-water.

The rock cycle

Materials from rocks are also used over and over again. This is called the **rock cycle**. It can take many millions of years:

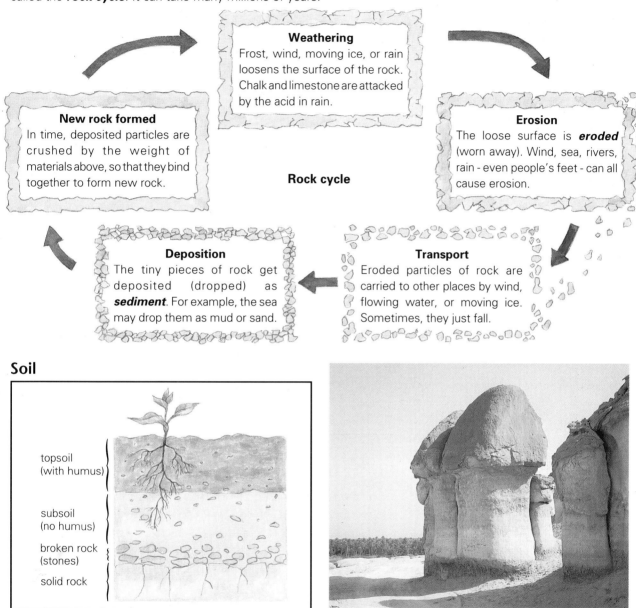

Weathering
Frost, wind, moving ice, or rain loosens the surface of the rock. Chalk and limestone are attacked by the acid in rain.

New rock formed
In time, deposited particles are crushed by the weight of materials above, so that they bind together to form new rock.

Rock cycle

Erosion
The loose surface is **eroded** (worn away). Wind, sea, rivers, rain - even people's feet - can all cause erosion.

Deposition
The tiny pieces of rock get deposited (dropped) as **sediment**. For example, the sea may drop them as mud or sand.

Transport
Eroded particles of rock are carried to other places by wind, flowing water, or moving ice. Sometimes, they just fall.

Soil

topsoil (with humus)

subsoil (no humus)

broken rock (stones)

solid rock

The effects of wind erosion

Soil is mainly formed from the rock underneath. The rock gets broken up by frost, rain, and expansion caused by the Sun's heat. The bigger fragments are **stones**. The smaller ones become the soil. Topsoil (the top layer) also contains decayed plant and animal remains. This is called **humus**. It is rich in the minerals which plants need for growth.

In some places, rivers deposit tiny rock particles as sediment. If the water retreats, this sediment becomes soil.

1 Explain how water from your tap can end up in a reservoir.
2 Cities have a huge demand for water. List the problems that this can cause.
3 What is *erosion*? What things can cause it?
4 Explain how particles worn away from one rock can end up as part of new rock.
5 Where does soil come from? How is it formed?

The Earth's rocks

By the end of this spread, you should be able to:
- describe the main types of rock found on Earth
- explain how these rocks are formed
- describe some uses of these rocks

The Earth was formed about 4500 million years ago from a cloud of very hot gas and dust around the Sun. Today, it is cooler, and mostly solid. But changes are still happening on its surface and beneath.

The Earth's structure

The core is mostly molten (melted) iron, though the inner core is kept solid by the great pressure there. Deep in the core, the temperature reaches 5000 °C.

The mantle is mostly solid rock made of silicates (compounds of silicon and oxygen). However, heat and pressure keep the material flexible, rather like Plasticine. Driven by heat from the core, it slowly circulates. Near the surface, any release of pressure turns it liquid. This hot, molten rock is called **magma**. Sometimes, it comes out of volcanoes as **lava**.

The crust is the thin, outer layer of the Earth. The continents are the thickest part (up to 90 km). They are mainly made of **granite**. They are like huge rafts which 'float' on the denser mantle underneath. Under the oceans, the crust is thinner (as little as 6 km). It is mainly a rock called **basalt**. In some places, the continental rafts push against each other. Here, the crust buckles and folds, forming mountain ranges.

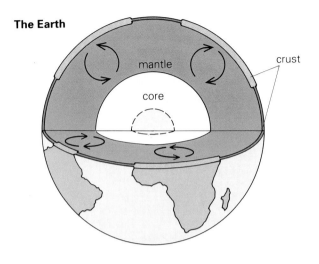

The Earth

Over millions of years, the shape of the crust slowly changes. The continental rafts move. Rocks are worn away by erosion. Pockets of magma become exposed. And rivers and seas advance and retreat.

Rocks in the crust

There are many different rocks in the Earth's crust, but they can be grouped into three main types:

Igneous rocks, such as granite and basalt, are made of tiny crystals. They are formed when molten magma cools and solidifies.

If magma cools *quickly*, the crystals are *small*. This happens when magma is exposed on the surface.

If magma cools *slowly*, the crystals have time to grow, and are *large*. This can happen to magma deep in the crust. It may take thousands of years for a large, pocket of magma to cool and solidify.

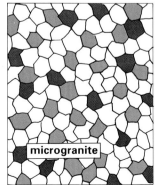

This rock cooled more quickly...   ......than this

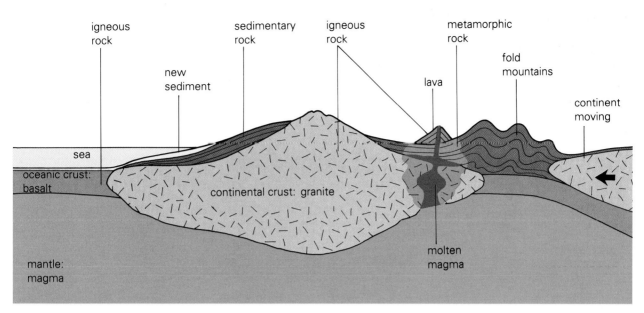

igneous rock · sedimentary rock · igneous rock · metamorphic rock · new sediment · lava · fold mountains · continent moving · sea · oceanic crust: basalt · continental crust: granite · molten magma · mantle: magma

Sedimentary rocks are formed from layers of sediment deposited by seas, rivers, wind, or moving ice. The sediments are compressed as more and more material collects above them. Then they harden, in much the same way as concrete sets. This process can take many millions of years. The layers of rock are called **strata**. You see them in sedimentary rocks such as **sandstone**, **limestone**, and **coal**.

Most sediments are particles of eroded rock. Sandstone is formed from sediments like this. However, some sediments are fragments of shells and bones from sea creatures which lived hundreds of millions of years ago. Limestone is usually formed in this way, though it can also be deposited chemically, like the scale in a kettle.

1. What is *magma*?
2. How are *igneous* rocks formed?
3. How can you tell whether an igneous rock cooled quickly or slowly when it formed?
4. How are *sedimentary* rocks formed?
5. a) Why do you think sedimentary rocks sometimes contain fossils? b) Why would you not expect to find fossils in a lump of granite?
6. What type of rock is *marble*? What was it originally, and how was it formed?
7. Some roofing tiles are made of slate. What would be the the advantages and disadvantages of using a) granite b) limestone instead?

Metamorphic rocks Deep underground, igneous and sedimentary rocks can be changed by heat or pressure or both. They become metamorphic ('changed') rock which is usually harder than the original. Examples include **marble** and **slate**:

Original rock		Metamorphic rock
limestone	$\xrightarrow{\text{heat}}$	marble
shale (mudstone)	$\xrightarrow{\text{pressure}}$	slate

Using rocks

Rocks are our source of minerals, such as diamond and gold. In fact the word 'mineral' really means anything useful that can be mined from the Earth. Here are some more uses of rocks:

Rock	Description	Examples of use
Granite	Very hard, sparkling	chippings, road stone building stone
Limestone	light colour	building/facing stone chippings in cement, concrete
Marble	light colour, hard, smooth	facing stone statues
Slate	hard, but splits into flat sheets	roofing tiles snooker tables

4·1 Electricity in action

By the end of this spread, you should be able to:
* *explain where electric charges come from, and how they affect each other*
* *explain how electric charge can be made to pass through some materials but not others*

Electricity from the atom

Electricity can make cling film stick to your hands. It can travel through wires. And it can light up the sky in a flash. But where does it come from? The answer is the atom:

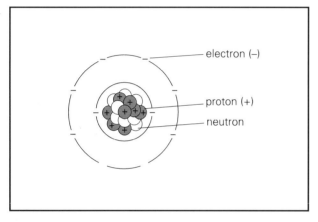

In an atom, there are two types of electric **charge** (see also Spread 3.8).**Electrons** have a **negative (–)** charge. **Protons** have a **positive (+)** charge. Atoms normally have the same number of electrons as protons, so, overall, they are uncharged.

Electrons do not always stay attached to atoms. When you switch on a light, the 'electricity' flowing through the wires is actually a flow of electrons:

A flow of electrons is called a **current**.
Put another way: a current is a flow of charge.

From conductors to insulators

Conductors are materials which let electrons flow through. In a conductor, some electrons are not very tightly held to their atoms. This means that they are free to move through the material.

Air and water can conduct, but only if they contain **ions** (see Spread 3.8). Ions are charged. In gases and liquids, they are free to move. So they can carry charge from one place to another.

Insulators are materials which do not let electrons flow through. Their electrons are held tightly to atoms, and are not free to move.

Semiconductors are 'inbetween' materials. They are insulators when cold, but conductors when warm. They are used in microchips (See Spread 4.4)

Conductors		Semiconductors	Insulators	
Good	*Poor*			
metals,	human body	silicon	plastics	glass
especially	water	germanium	e.g.	rubber
silver	air		PVC	
copper			polystyrene	
aluminium			Perspex	
carbon				

Static electricity

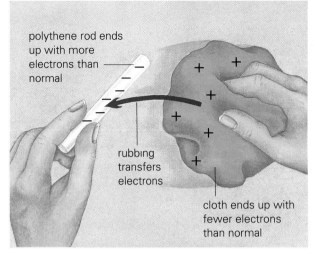

polythene rod ends up with more electrons than normal

rubbing transfers electrons

cloth ends up with fewer electrons than normal

Insulators can become charged when rubbed. People say that they have 'static electricity' on them.

If you rub a polythene rod with a cloth, the polythene pulls electrons from the cloth. The polythene ends up negatively (–) charged, and the cloth positively (+) charged.

If you rub Perspex with a cloth, the effect is opposite: the cloth pulls electrons from the Perspex.

The rubbing action doesn't make electric charge. It just separates charges already there. It works with insulators because, once the charges are separated, they tend to stay where they are.

Forces between charges If charged rods are held close, there are forces between them:

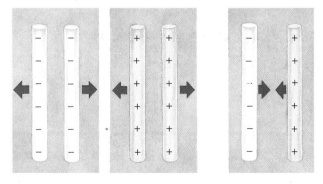

Like charges repel. Unlike charges attract.

A charge will also attract something uncharged. That is why dust is attracted to the charged screen of a TV. Being uncharged, the dust has equal amounts of + and –, so it feels attraction and repulsion. But the attracted charges are pulled slightly nearer the screen, so the force on them is stronger.

Battery and circuit

A **battery** can make electrons move. But there must be a conducting material between its two **terminals**. Then, a chemical reaction inside the battery will push electrons out of the negative (–) terminal and round to the positive (+) terminal.

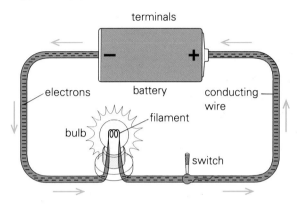

terminals

electrons   battery   conducting wire

filament

bulb   switch

The battery above is being used to light up a bulb. The conducting path through the bulb, wires, switch, and battery is called a **circuit**. As the electrons pass through the bulb, they make a **filament** (thin wire) heat up so that it glows.

There must be a *complete* circuit for the current to flow. If the circuit is broken, the flow of electrons stops, and the bulb goes out. Turning the switch OFF breaks the circuit by separating two contacts.

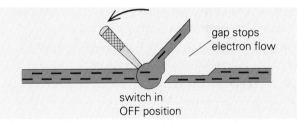

gap stops electron flow

switch in OFF position

1. Which materials are the best conductors?
2. What type of charge is there on an electron?
3. Explain why you think electrons are pushed out of the negative (–) terminal of a battery and not the positive (+).
4. If you rub Perspex with a cloth, electrons are transferred from the Perspex to the cloth. What type of charge does this leave a) on the Perspex b) on the cloth?
5. A circuit contains a bulb, battery, and switch. Explain why the bulb stops working if you turn off the switch.

Batteries and bulbs

By the end of this spread, you should be able to:
- *explain how current and voltage are measured*
- *describe the differences between series and parallel circuits*

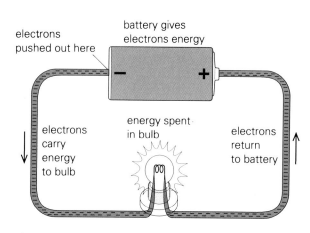

In the circuit above, the battery is *giving* the electrons energy as it pushes them out. The electrons are *spending* this energy when they flow through the bulb. The energy is given off as heat and light. (For more on energy, see Spread 4.7).

Current

Current is measured in **amperes** (**A**). The higher the current, the greater the flow of electrons.

Current is measured with an **ammeter**, connected into the circuit like this:

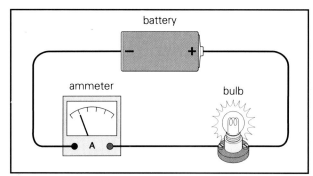

The ammeter can be connected anywhere in this circuit because the current is the same all the way round. Putting in the ammeter doesn't affect the flow of electricity.

Small currents are sometimes measured in **milliamperes** (**mA**). 1000 mA = 1 A

Voltage

Batteries have a **voltage** marked on the side. It is measured in **volts** (**V**). The higher the voltage, the more energy each electron is given - so the more energy it has to spend as it flows round the circuit.

The voltage of a battery can be measured by connecting a voltmeter across the terminals:

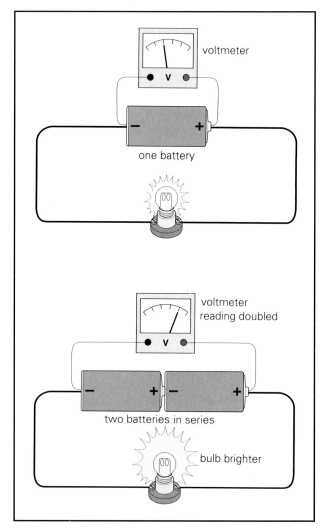

If *two* batteries are connected in **series** (in a line), the total voltage is twice what it was before. Also, the bulb glows more brightly because a higher current is pushed through it:

- The more batteries are connected in series, the higher the voltage.
- The higher the voltage across a bulb, the higher the current flowing though.

Series and parallel

Here are two different ways of adding an extra bulb to the previous circuit:

Bulbs in series The bulbs glow dimly. It is more difficult for the the electrons to pass through two bulbs than one, so there is less current than before.

Adding more bulbs makes them even dimmer. And if *one* bulb is removed, the circuit is broken. So *all* the bulbs go out.

Bulbs in parallel The bulbs glow brightly, because each is getting the full battery voltage. However, together, two bright bulbs take more current than a single bright bulb, so the battery will not last as long.

If one bulb is removed, there is still a complete circuit through the other bulb, so it keeps glowing brightly.

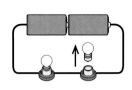

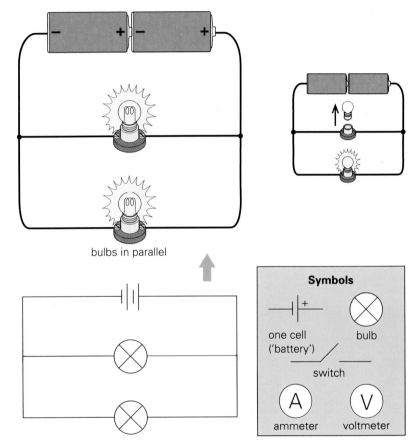

bulbs in series

bulbs in parallel

Circuit symbols

It can take a long time to draw pictures of circuits! That is why scientists and electricians prefer to use **symbols**.

On the right, you can see the parallel bulb circuit, drawn using symbols.

Symbols

one cell ('battery')

bulb

switch

ammeter

voltmeter

1 In the circuit on the right, what type of meter is X? What reading would you expect to see on it?
2 What type of meter is Y?
3 Redraw the circuit, so that it has two batteries instead of one, and Y is across both. What difference would you expect to see in a) the brightness of the bulb b) the reading on X c) the reading on Y?
4 If an extra bulb is added to your new circuit in *series*, how will this affect a) the brightness b) the current?
5 What are the advantages of connecting the extra bulb in *parallel*?

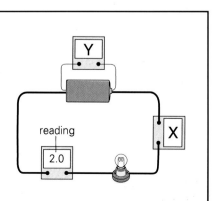

reading

2.0

Resistance and energy

By the end of this spread, you should be able to:
- *describe some of the effects of resistance*
- *calculate the cost of running different electrical appliances at home*

Resistance and resistors

Bulbs do not conduct as well as connecting wire. Scientists say that they have more **resistance** to electricity. Energy has to be spent overcoming this resistance. The bulb gives off this energy as heat and light.

The more resistance there is in a circuit, the lower the current.

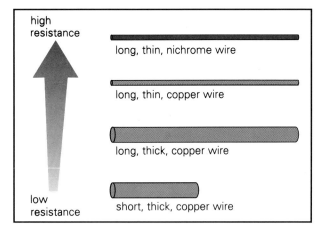

Some metals have less resistance then others. In circuits, the connecting wires are usually made of copper because it has low resistance. The thickness and length of the wire also affects the resistance.

Resistors are specially designed to provide resistance. They are used in electronics circuits so that the right amount of current is fed to different components (parts) to make them work properly.

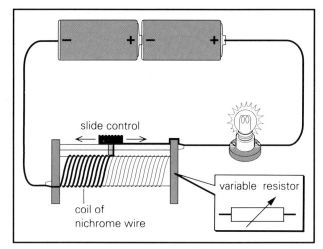

Above, a **variable resistor** is being used to control the brightness of a bulb. The variable resistor contains a long coil of thin nichrome wire. Sliding the control to the right puts more resistance into the circuit, so the bulb gets dimmer.

Heat from resistance

Whenever current flows through a resistance, heat is given off. This idea is used in the filament of a light bulb. It is also used in the **heating elements** in **appliances** such as kettles, irons, and toasters. The elements normally contain lengths of nichrome wire.

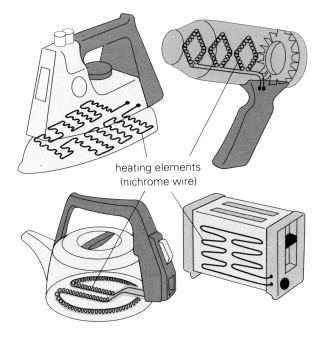

heating elements
(nichrome wire)

Paying for energy

Most appliances get their energy from the **mains**. This energy has to be paid for.

Appliances usually have a **power** marked on them, in **watts (W)** or in **kilowatts (kW)**. There are some examples on the right. The higher the power, the quicker the appliance takes energy from the mains. (For more on energy and power, see 4.7 and 4.14).

The energy supplied depends on the power of the appliance *and* on how long it is switched on for. Electricity Boards measure energy in **kilowatt hours (kW h)**, also called **units**. For example:

If 1 kW is switched on for 1 hour, then 1 kW h of energy is supplied.

If 2 kW is switched on for 3 hour, then 6 kW h of energy is supplied.

These results can be worked out with an equation:

energy	=	power	×	time
in kW h		in watts		in hours

Electricity Boards charge for each kW h (unit). On the right, you can see how to calculate the cost of running an appliance.

If the power is given in watts, you must change this into kilowatts before using the equation.
1 kW = 1000 W. So, for example, 100 W = 0.1 kW.

Reading the meter

Every house has an 'electricity meter'. Really, it is an energy meter. Below, you can see how the meter reading in one house changed over a 24-hour period. To work out how many units (kW h) were supplied, you take one number from the other.

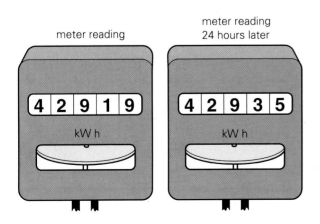

meter reading

meter reading 24 hours later

Typical powers			
in kW		**in W**	
kettle	2.4	vacuum cleaner	600
fan heater	2	electric drill	500
hairdrier	2	food mixer	500
hotplate	1.5	colour TV	120
iron	1	table lamp	60
toaster	1	stereo	60

1 kW = 1000 W

Using a 3 kW heater for 4 hours

Energy = power × time
= 3 kW × 4 h
= 12 kW h

The Electricity Board charges 10p per kW h (unit). So,

cost = 12 × 10p
= 120p
= £1.20

1 Why is thick copper better than thin for connecting wire? Why would you not use nichrome for connecting wire?

2 What is nichrome wire used for? Why?

3 In the circuit at the top of the opposite page, what will happen to the bulb if the variable resistor control is moved to the *left*? Why?

The table on this page gives the powers of some appliances. Assume that energy costs 10p per unit:

4 How much energy (in kW h) is needed to run the toaster for 2 hours? What will it cost?

5 What is the cost of running a) the fan heater for 4 hours b) the food mixer for 2 hours?

6 Use the meter readings on the left to work out the cost of the energy supplied.

4·4 Switches and gates

By the end of this spread, you should be able to:
- *explain what sensors are, and how they can be used to control electronic switches*
- *explain how logic gates can be used*

You turn ordinary switches on and off with your fingers. However, **electronic switches** are turned on and off by tiny electric currents. Electronic switches are normally in **microchips** like the one on the right. A single 'chip' contains several switches.

**microchip
(containing logic gates)**

Sensors

The current which controls an electronic switch comes from a **sensor**. Sensors detect heat, light, sound, pressure from your finger, or some other **stimulus** from the outside world.

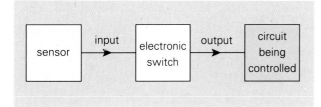

This **flow diagram** shows what happens. The electronic switch gets an **input** (a tiny current) from the sensor. As a result, it produces an **output** (it is either ON or OFF).

Here are some jobs for electronic switches:

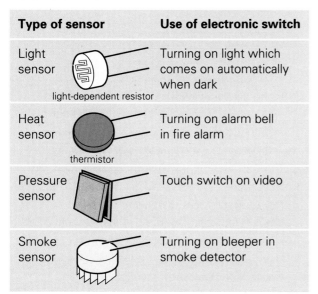

Type of sensor	Use of electronic switch
Light sensor *light-dependent resistor*	Turning on light which comes on automatically when dark
Heat sensor *thermistor*	Turning on alarm bell in fire alarm
Pressure sensor	Touch switch on video
Smoke sensor	Turning on bleeper in smoke detector

Electronic switches can only handle tiny currents. So they cannot directly switch on powerful things, like electric motors and alarm bells. To get round this problem, a **relay** is used (see the next spread, 4.5). The electronic switch turns on the relay, and this switches on the more powerful circuit.

Logic gates

Switches can be grouped together to make **logic gates**. Here is a simple logic gate, a box containing two switches in series:

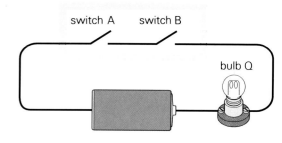

With this gate:
If A *and* B are ON, the bulb is ON,
but if either A or B is OFF, the bulb is OFF.

You can use a **truth table** to show the results of all the switch settings. The table uses two **logic numbers**: *0* for **OFF**, and *1* for **ON** :

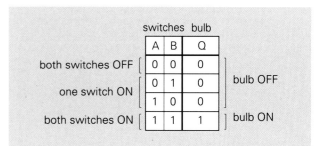

	switches		bulb
	A	B	Q
both switches OFF	0	0	0
one switch ON	0	1	0
	1	0	0
both switches ON	1	1	1

bulb OFF / bulb ON

Electronic switches are used in most logic gates. The chip at the top of the page contains logic gates.

Here are three types of logic gate:

AND gate

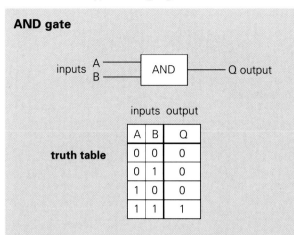

inputs A B — AND — Q output

truth table

inputs		output
A	B	Q
0	0	0
0	1	0
1	0	0
1	1	1

The output is only ON if both inputs are on.
In other words, Q is ON if A *AND* B are ON.

OR gate

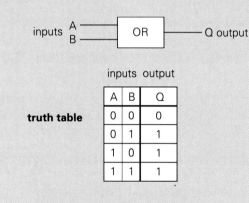

inputs A B — OR — Q output

truth table

inputs		output
A	B	Q
0	0	0
0	1	1
1	0	1
1	1	1

The output is ON if either input is ON.
In other words, Q is ON if A *OR* B is ON.

NOT gate

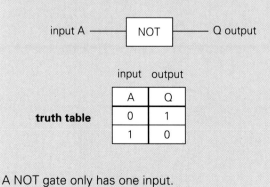

input A — NOT — Q output

truth table

input	output
A	Q
0	1
1	0

A NOT gate only has one input.
The output is ON if the input is OFF, and vice versa.
In other words, Q is ON if A is *NOT* ON.

Using sensors and gates

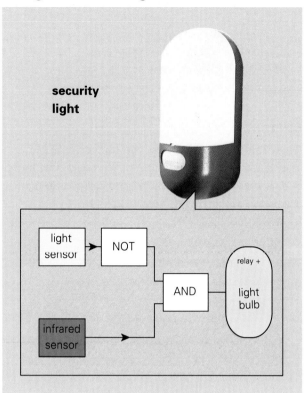

security light

This security light uses sensors and logic gates. If it is dark, and someone approaches, the light switches on automatically.

The *light sensor* detects whether it is light or dark.
The *infrared sensor* detects body heat.

The gates are connected so that:
- the bulb is OFF if the light sensor is ON (in other words, if it is daytime).
- the bulb is ON if the light sensor is OFF *and* the infrared sensor is ON (in other words, if it is dark, *and* someone is approaching).

The NOT gate 'reverses' the effect of the light sensor. Without it, the light would only work in the daytime!

1 If you have two ordinary switches in series, what type of logic gate do they make?
2 With an OR gate, what input settings are needed so that the output is OFF.
3 What effect does a NOT gate have?
4 What type of gate would you use in
   a) a safe which will only open if two buttons are pressed at once? b) a door which can be opened by either of two buttons?

Magnets and electromagnets

By the end of this spread, you should be able to:
- describe the effects of magnets and electromagnets
- explain some of the uses of electromagnets

Magnets

A few metals are **magnetic**. They are attracted to magnets and can be magnetized. The main magnetic metals are iron and steel (but not stainless steel).

The force from a magnet seems to come from two points near the ends. These are called the **north pole (N)** and the **south pole (S)** of the magnet.

When the poles of a magnet are brought close, you can feel a force between them:

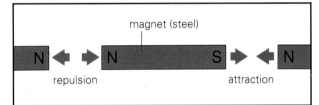

Like poles repel. Unlike poles attract.

Magnetic fields

A magnet will push or pull on other magnets, and attract unmagnetized pieces of iron and steel nearby. Scientists say that the magnet has a **magnetic field** around it. You can use a **compass**, to see the direction of the forces from this field. (A compass is a tiny magnet which is free to turn on a spindle and line up with the field.)

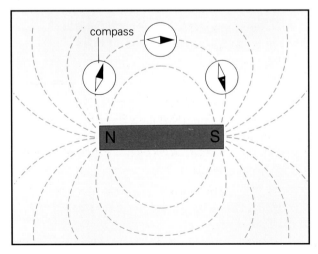

Electromagnets

If a current flows through a wire, there is a magnetic field around the wire. All currents produce a magnetic field. The effect is used in an **electromagnet**.

The electromagnet below produces a field rather like the one around a bar magnet. Without the iron **core**, it would still produce a field, but the iron makes the field much stronger. The field is even stronger if
- the current is increased
- there are more turns on the coil

The iron core becomes magnetized when the electromagnet is switched on. It *loses* its magnetism when the electromagnet is switched off. However, a steel core would *keep* its magnetism. This idea is used to make magnets.

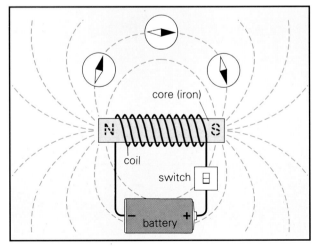

Using electromagnets

These devices all make use of electromagnets:

Relay This is a switch operated by an electromagnet. With a relay, it is possible to use a tiny switch with thin wires to turn on the current in a much more powerful circuit - for example, a mains circuit with a big electric motor in it.

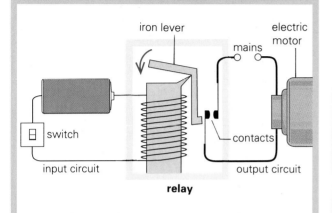

relay

How it works If you switch on the current in the input circuit, the electromagnet pulls on an iron lever. This closes two contacts in the output circuit.

Circuit breaker This is an automatic safety switch. It cuts off the current in a circuit if this gets too high.

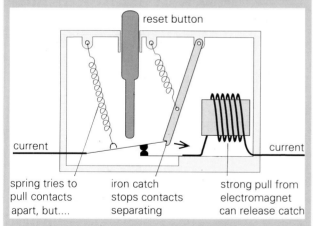

spring tries to pull contacts apart, but....   iron catch stops contacts separating   strong pull from electromagnet can release catch

How it works The current flows through two contacts and also through an electromagnet. A spring is trying to pull the contacts apart, but there is an iron catch stopping them from opening. If the current gets too high, the pull of the electromagnet becomes strong enough to release the catch, so the contacts open.

Loudspeaker This has a cone, usually made of paper, which makes the air in front of it vibrate. When these vibrations reach your ears, you hear them as sound (see also Spread 4.15).

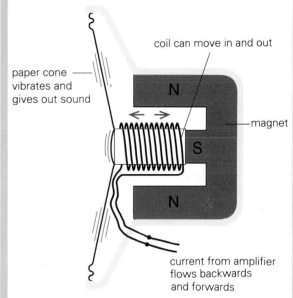

How it works The cone is attached to a coil which is in the field of a magnet. The **amplifier** in your radio or stereo gives out a current which flows backwards, forwards, backwards, forwards..... and so on, through the coil. The coil pushes and pulls on the magnet. This makes the coil move in and out, so the cone vibrates.

---

1 How can you show that there is a magnetic field around a magnet?
2 What changes would you make to an electromagnet to give it a stronger pull?
3 Describe how you could magnetize a steel nail.
4 Explain why, with a relay, it only takes a small current to switch on an electric motor, even though the motor takes a big current.
5 Explain why a circuit breaker will not cut off the current until this passes a certain level.
6 Explain why a loudspeaker uses current which goes backwards, forwards, backwards, forwards ... and so on.

Turning and changing

By the end of this spread, you should be able to:
- *explain how a simple electric motor works*
- *explain how electricity is generated*
- *explain what transformers can be used for*

Electric motors

A current produces a magnetic field, so it feels the force of a magnet. In an electric motor, this force is used to produce a turning effect.

The diagram on the right shows a simple electric motor. The motor has a coil which can spin between the poles of a magnet. The coil is supplied with current through two contacts called **brushes**.

The current makes the coil become an electromagnet. Its poles feel forces from the poles either side. The coil flips round until *unlike* poles are facing.....

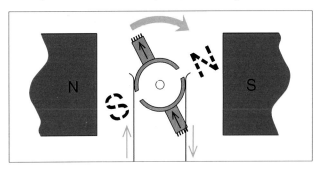

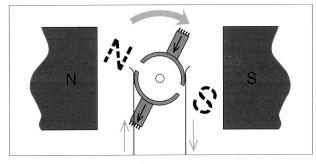

.....but as the coil passes through the vertical, the **commutator**, reverses the current. This reverses the poles of the coil. Now, *like* poles are facing each other, and repelling. So the coil flips round another half-turn until *unlike* poles are facing. Then the commutator reverses the current again....... and so on. In this way, the motor keeps turning.

Practical motors often use electromagnets rather than ordinary magnets. Also, for smoother running, they usually have several coils set at different angles.

Simple electric motor

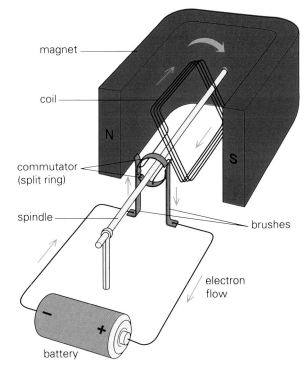

Generators, AC, and DC

If you take a simple electric motor, remove the battery, replace it with a meter, and spin the coil, the motor *produces* an electric current. It has become a **generator**.

Michael Faraday discovered how to generate electricity, in 1831. He found that whenever wires cut through a magnetic field, or are in a changing magnetic field, then a voltage is produced. The faster the change, the higher the voltage.

Most modern generators are **alternators**. The current they produce *alternates* in direction: it flows backwards, forwards, backwards, forwards ....and so on as the generator turns. Current like this is called **alternating current (AC)**. For example, the electricity which comes from the mains is AC. It flows backwards and forwards 50 times every second. In some equipment, this causes a slight hum.

The current from a battery always flows in the same direction. It is called **direct current (DC)**.

Simple alternator

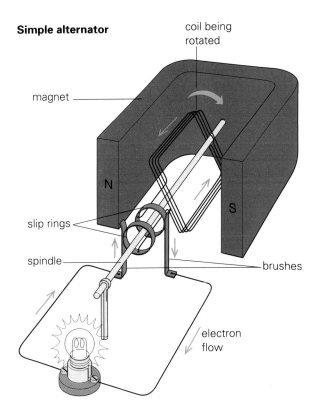

In the alternator above, the brushes rub against two metal *slip rings*. As the coil faces first one way and then the other, the current generated in the coil flows backwards and then forwards. This makes alternating current flow through the bulb.

Mains electricity comes from huge alternators in power stations (see spreads 4.9 and 4.10). The alternators have fixed coils round the outside with rotating electromagnets in the middle.

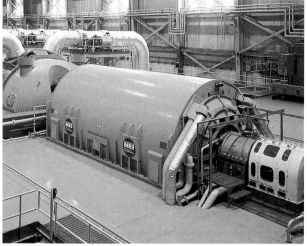

Alternator in a power station

Transformers

Transformers can change the voltage of an alternating current. For example, they can be used to reduce the 230 volts mains voltage to the 9 volts or so needed for the electronic circuits in radios, cassette players, and video games.

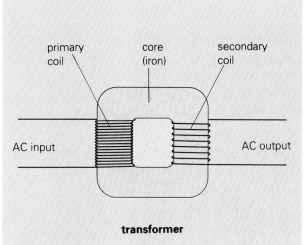

transformer

Transformers make use of Faraday's discovery that a changing magnetic field can generate a voltage. The *primary coil* is as an electromagnet. Connected to an AC supply, it produces an alternating magnetic field. This generates AC in the *secondary coil*.

For the right output voltage, the coils have to be carefully chosen. For example, if the number of secondary turns is half the number of primary turns, then the output voltage is half the input voltage.

A transformer alone is not enough to power low-voltage electronic circuits. Extra components are needed to change the transformer's AC output into the DC needed by the circuits.

---

1 In an electric motor, what job is done by
   a) the brushes b) the commutator?
2 Suggest *three* ways in which you could make an electric motor give a stronger turning effect.
3 What is the difference between *alternating current* and *direct current*? Which type comes from a) a battery b) the mains c) an alternator?
4 In a simple alternator a) how is the current generated? b) what are the slip rings for?
5 What are transformers used for? Which type of current do they use, *AC* or *DC*?

Spending energy

By the end of this spread, you should be able to:
- *describe some different forms of energy*
- *name a unit for measuring energy*
- *explain what happens when energy changes form*
- *give some examples of energy changing form*

You spend **energy** when you climb the stairs, lift a bag, or hit a tennis ball. Energy is spent whenever a force moves. The greater the force, and the further it moves, the more energy is spent.

There is more on the link between force and energy in Spread 4.14.

Energy and its forms

Energy has several different forms:

Kinetic energy means 'movement energy'. A moving thing has energy because it can make forces move when it hits something else.

Potential energy means 'stored energy'. Lift something up, and you give it potential energy. The energy is stored until you drop it. Stretch a spring, and you give it potential energy.

Chemical energy This is really another type of stored energy. Foods, fuels, and batteries have chemical energy. The energy is released by chemical reactions.

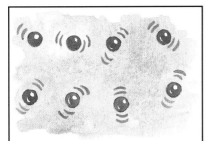

Heat energy Everything is made of particles (such as atoms). These are constantly on the move, so they have energy. The higher the temperature, the faster they move, and the more energy they have. If a hot thing cools down, its particles lose energy. The energy given out is called heat.

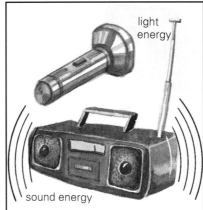

Radiant energy Light and sound carry energy as they radiate from their source.

Electrical energy Electrons have electrical energy when they are pushed out from the terminal of a battery.

Nuclear energy is stored in the nucleus of the atom. It is released by nuclear reactions.

Energy is measured in **joules (J)**.

On the right, you can see some examples of different amounts of energy. Large amounts are sometimes measured in **kilojoules (kJ)**. 1 kJ = 1000 J.

Energy chains

Just like money, energy doesn't vanish when you spend it. It just goes somewhere else! Below is an example of how energy can change from one form to another. Scientists call it an **energy chain**:

In every energy chain, the *total amount* of energy stays the same. Scientists express this idea in the *law of conservation of energy*:

Energy can change into different forms, but it cannot be made or destroyed.

Typical energy values	
Potential energy:	
stretched rubber band	1 J
you, on top of a step-ladder	500 J
Kinetic energy:	
kicked football	50 J
small car at 70 mph	500 000 J
Heat energy:	
hot cup of tea	150 000 J
Chemical energy:	
torch battery	10 000 J
chocolate biscuit	300 000 J
litre of petrol	35 000 000 J

| chemical energy | → | kinetic energy | → | potential energy | → | kinetic energy | → | heat energy |

In any chain, some energy is always wasted as heat. For example, you give off heat when you exercise, which is why you sweat! However, the *total* amount of energy (including the heat) stays the same.

1. Give an example of something which has a) kinetic energy b) chemical energy c) potential energy.
2. A fire gives out 10 kJ of energy. What is this in joules?
3. What type of energy is supplied to a car engine? What happens to this energy?
4. Describe the energy changes which take place when you apply the brakes on a moving cycle.
5. Describe the energy changes which take place when you throw a ball up into the air.
6. Scientists say that energy can 'never be destroyed'. Explain what they mean.

Energy changers

Here are some energy changers in action:

Energy input	Energy changer	Energy output
electrical energy	→ heating element →	heat energy
sound energy	→ microphone →	electrical energy
electrical energy	→ loudspeaker →	sound energy
kinetic energy	→ brakes →	heat energy

Heat on the move

By the end of this spread, you should be able to:
- *describe three ways in which heat can travel*
- *explain how different materials can be used to cut down the movement of heat*

Everything is made of particles (such as atoms) which are constantly on the move. If something hot cools down, its particles lose energy. The energy given out is called **heat**. It can travel in three ways:

Conduction

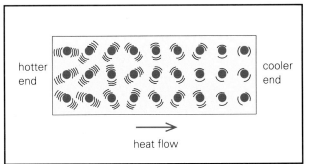

hotter end

cooler end

heat flow

If one end of a bar is heated, its particles vibrate faster. In time, their extra movement is passed on to particles right along the bar. Scientists say that heat is travelling by **conduction**.

Metals are the best conductors of heat. This is because their atoms have some 'loose' electrons which can quickly carry energy from one part of the metal to another. These same electrons also make metals good conductors of electricity.

Poor conductors of heat are called **insulators**.

Good conductors	Insulators (poor conductors)	
metals	glass	
especially:	water	
silver	plastic	⎡ wool
copper	wood	fibrewool
aluminium	materials with air trapped in them	plastic foam
		fur
	air	feathers ⎦

Air is a poor conductor of heat. Feathers, fibrewool, plastic foam, wool, and fur are all good insulators because they contain tiny pockets of trapped air.

Convection

If air is heated, it expands, and floats upwards. Cooler, denser air moves in to take its place. The result is a circulating flow called a **convection current**. Convection can occur in other gases as well as air. And it can occur in liquids, such as water.

Most rooms are heated by convection:

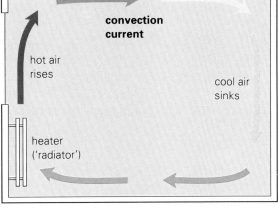

air cools

convection current

hot air rises

cool air sinks

heater ('radiator')

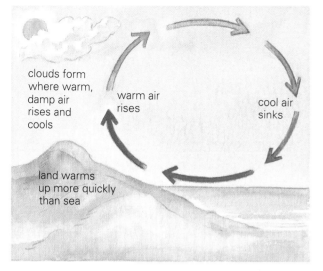

clouds form where warm, damp air rises and cools

warm air rises

cool air sinks

land warms up more quickly than sea

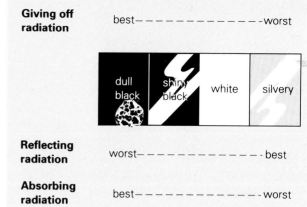

Convection has a part to play in the weather. You can see an example above. During the day, the land warms up more quickly than the sea. This sets up a convection current so that breezes blow in from the sea. Where warm, damp air rises and cools, clouds may form (see Spread 3.15).

Radiation

There is empty space between us and the Sun. But we still get heat from the Sun. The energy travels as tiny waves of *electromagnetic radiation* (see Spread 4.19). These can travel through empty space.

If you absorb any of the Sun's radiation, it heats you up. That is why it is sometimes called *heat radiation*. Often, people just call it 'radiation', though their are other types of radiation as well.

Everything gives off some heat radiation. The hotter it is, the more it radiates.

---

1   Why can the Sun's heat not reach us by conduction or convection? How does the Sun's heat reach us?
2   How can a heater warm a room by convection?
3   Explain why a) insulating materials often contain trapped air b) houses in hot countries are often painted white c) kettles are usually silvery or white.
4   What features does a Thermos flask have to stop heat losses by a) conduction b) convection c) radiation? Why is a flask good at keeping drinks cold as well as hot?

Black surfaces are the best at giving off radiation. They are also the best at absorbing it.

Silvery or white surfaces are good at reflecting radiation - which means that they are poor at absorbing it. In hot, sunny countries, buildings are often painted white so that they absorb as little of the Sun's radiation as possible.

Silvery or white surfaces are also poor at giving off radiation. Kettles are usually made silvery or white so that they lose heat slowly.

The Thermos flask

A Thermos flask can keep drinks hot (or cold) for hours. It has several features which reduce the amount of heat flowing out (or in):

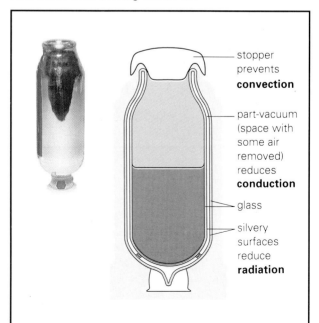

stopper prevents **convection**

part-vacuum (space with some air removed) reduces **conduction**

glass

silvery surfaces reduce **radiation**

Fuels and energy

By the end of this spread and the next (4.10), you should be able to:
- *explain how the world gets its energy*
- *describe some of the problems caused by using fuels, and give some alternatives*
- *explain what efficiency means*

Industrial societies need huge amounts of energy. Most come from fuels which are burnt in power stations, factories, homes, and vehicles. Fuels are a very concentrated source of energy. For example, there is enough energy in a teaspoonful of petrol to move a large car more than 50 metres. Our fuel, food, is also a very concentrated source of energy.

Most of the world's energy originally came from the Sun. To find out how, see the next spread.

Turbine

Power stations

Mains electricity comes from generators in power stations. In many power stations, the generators are turned by **turbines**, blown round by the force of high pressure steam (see below). For other ways of turning generators, see the next spread.

Engines

Engines get their energy from burning fuel. For example, in a car engine, a mixture of fuel and air is exploded. This provides the force which turns the engine. When an engine is running fast, there can be more than 25 explosions per second in each cylinder.

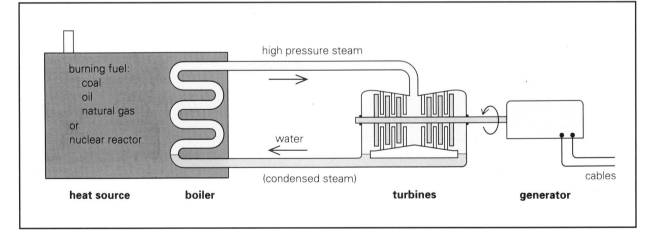

Burning fuels

Fuels use up oxygen when they burn. With most fuels (including food), this reaction takes place:

fuel + oxygen → carbon dioxide + water

There may be other products as well. For example burning coal produces some sulphur dioxide.

Using fuels brings many problems. For example:
- Carbon dioxide gas adds to global warming.
- Sulphur dioxide causes acid rain.
- Transporting fuels can cause pollution: for example, there may be a leak from an oil tanker.
- Supplies of most fuels will eventually run out.

Renewable or non-renewable?

Coal, oil, and natural gas are called **fossil fuels** (see the next spread). They took many millions of years to form. Once used up, they cannot be replaced. They are **non-renewable**.

Some fuels are **renewable**. For example, if wood is burnt, it can be replaced by growing more trees.

You can see some examples of renewable and non-renewable energy sources below. For more details on each one, see the next spread.

Non-renewable energy sources	Renewable energy sources
fossil fuels:	hydroelectric energy
coal	tidal energy
oil	wave energy
natural gas	wind energy
	solar energy
nuclear fuel:	geothermal energy
uranium-235	biofuels (fuels from plant and animal matter)

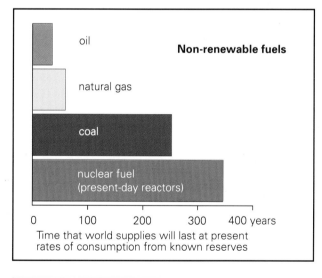

Non-renewable fuels

oil

natural gas

coal

nuclear fuel (present-day reactors)

0   100   200   300   400 years

Time that world supplies will last at present rates of consumption from known reserves

Efficiency

When fuels burn, much of their energy is wasted as heat. In a typical power station for example, for every 100 joules of energy in the fuel, only 35 joules ends up as electrical energy. The power station has an **efficiency** of 35%.

You can use this equation to work out efficiency:

$$\text{efficiency} = \frac{\text{energy output}}{\text{energy input}} \times 100\%$$

Here are some typical efficiency values:

For every **100 J** of Input energy		Output energy	Efficiency
petrol engine		25 J	25%
diesel engine		35 J	35%
fuel-burning power station		35 J	35%
human engine		15 J	15%

Low efficiency is not because of poor design. When an engine is working, some energy *has* to be wasted. Burning fuel gives particles extra energy. But some of this becomes so spread out that it cannot be used to produce motion. Instead, it is lost as heat.

In some power stations, wasted heat is used to supply the local district with hot water. This is just one way of being less wasteful with fuel so that the world's reserves last longer.

To answer the following, you may need information from Spread 4.10

1 Some fuels are *non-renewable*. What does this mean? Give *two* examples.

2 Describe *two* problems which can be caused by gases from burning fuels.

3 Give *two* ways of generating electricity in which no fuel is burnt and the energy is renewable.

4 The energy in petrol originally came from the Sun. Explain how it got into the petrol.

5 A petrol engine has an efficiency of 25%. Explain what this means.

6 Why it is important for engines and power stations to have the highest possible efficiency?

How the world gets its energy

Solar panels

These absorb energy radiated from the Sun and use it to heat water.

Solar cells

These use the energy in sunlight to produce small amounts of electricity.

The Sun

The Sun radiates energy because of nuclear reactions deep inside it. Its output is equivalent to 400 million billion billion electric fire elements. Just a tiny fraction reaches the Earth.

Energy in food

We get energy from the food we eat. The food may be from plants, or from animals which fed on plants.

Energy in plants

Plants take in energy from sunlight falling on their leaves. They use it to turn water and carbon dioxide from the air into new growth. Animals eat plants to get the energy stored in them.

Biofuels from plants

Wood is still an important fuel in many countries. When wood is burnt, it releases energy which the tree once took in from the Sun. In some countries, sugar cane is grown and fermented to make alcohol, which can be used as a fuel instead of petrol.

Fossil fuels

Coal, oil, and natural gas are called fossil fuels. They were formed from the remains of plants and tiny sea creatures which lived many millions of years ago. Industrial societies rely on fossil fuels for most of their energy. Many power stations burn fossil fuels.

Biofuels from waste

Rotting animal and plant waste can give off methane gas (the same as natural gas). This can be used as a fuel. Marshes, rubbish tips, and sewage treatment works are all sources of methane. Some waste can also be used directly as fuel by burning it.

Batteries

Some batteries (e.g. car batteries) have to be given energy by charging them with electricity. Others are manufactured from chemicals which already store energy. But energy is needed to produce the chemicals in the first place.

Fuels from oil

Many fuels can be extracted from oil (crude). These include: petrol, diesel fuel, jet fuel, paraffin, central heating oil, bottled gas.

The Moon
The gravitational pull of the Moon (and to a lesser extent, the Sun) creates gentle bulges in the Earth's oceans. As the Earth rotates, different places have high and low tides as they pass in and out of the bulges.

Tidal energy
In a tidal energy scheme, an estuary is dammed to form an artificial lake. Incoming tides fills the lake; outgoing tides empty it. The flow of water in and out of the lake turns generators.

The atom
Some atoms have huge amounts of nuclear energy, stored in their nuclei (centres). Radioactive materials have unstable atoms which release energy slowly. Nuclear reactors can release energy much more quickly.

Nuclear power
In a reactor, nuclear reactions release energy from nuclei of uranium atoms. This produces heat which is used to make steam for driving generators.

Geothermal energy
Deep underground, the rocks are hotter than they are on the surface. The heat comes from radioactive materials naturally present in the rocks. It can be used to make steam for heating buildings or driving generators.

Weather systems
These are driven by heat radiated from the Sun. Hot air rising above the equator causes belts of wind around the Earth. Heat and winds lift water vapour from the oceans and bring rain and snow.

Wave energy
Waves are caused by the wind (and partly by tides). Waves cause a rapid up-and-down movement on the surface of the sea. This movement can be used to drive generators.

Hydroelectric energy
An artificial lake forms behind a dam. Water rushing down from this lake is used to turn generators. The lake is kept full by river water which once fell as rain or snow.

Wind energy
For centuries, people have been using the power of the wind to move ships, pump water, and grind corn. Today, huge wind turbines are used to turn electrical generators.

Forces and pressure

By the end of this spread, you should be able to:
• describe some effects of forces
• explain what pressure is and how to calculate it

Forces in action

A force is a push or pull. It is measured in **newtons (N)**.

On Earth, everything has **weight**, the downward force of gravity. Like other forces, weight is measured in newtons.

On Earth, a 1 kg mass has a weight of about 10 newtons. The force can be measured using a **newtonmeter**. This has a spring inside. The greater the force, the more the spring stretches and the further the pointer moves along the scale:

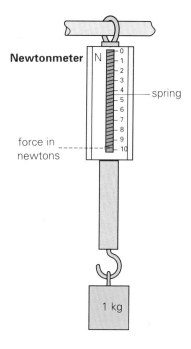

Newtonmeter

spring

force in newtons

1 kg

Forces can make things
• speed up
• slow down
• change shape
• turn
• move in a different direction

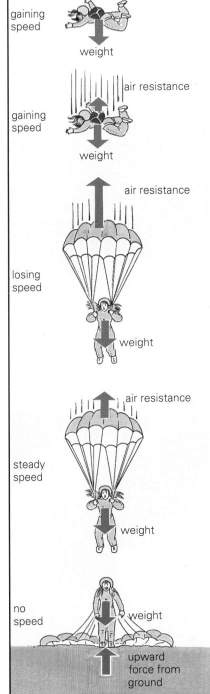

gaining speed

weight

gaining speed

air resistance

weight

air resistance

losing speed

weight

air resistance

steady speed

weight

no speed

weight

upward force from ground

A skydiver jumps from a helicopter. Weight is the only force acting on her. It makes her **accelerate** (gain speed).

As she gains speed, the force of **air resistance** gets stronger and stronger.

When she opens her parachute, there is a sudden increase in air resistance. So she loses speed until....

the air resistance equals her weight. Now, the two forces are in balance. The **resultant** force on the skydiver is zero, and her speed is steady.

The skydiver stands on the ground. The ground is slightly compressed by her feet. It provides an upward force equal to her weight. This force stops her sinking into the ground.

Pressure

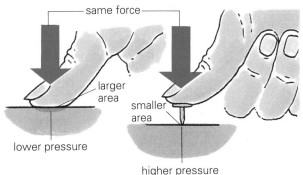

same force

larger area

smaller area

lower pressure

higher pressure

You can't push your thumb into wood. But you can push a drawing pin in using the same force. This is because the force is concentrated on a much smaller area. Scientists say that the **pressure** is higher.

Pressure is measured in **newtons per square metre (N/m²)**, also called **pascals (Pa)**. It can be calculated with this equation:

$$\text{pressure} = \frac{\text{force}}{\text{area}}$$

force in N
area in m²
pressure in Pa

For example:

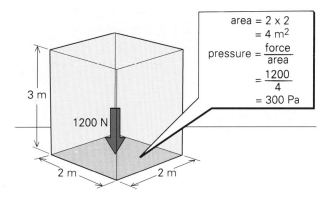

3 m

1200 N

2 m   2 m

area = 2 x 2
     = 4 m²
pressure = $\frac{\text{force}}{\text{area}}$
         = $\frac{1200}{4}$
         = 300 Pa

1. Sara has a mass of 50 kg. What is her weight?
2. Sara is using a parachute. She is descending at steady speed. Draw a diagram to show the forces on her. What is the resultant force?
3. Use your ideas about pressure to explain why
   a) it is easier to walk on soft sand if you have flat shoes rather than shoes with small heels.
   b) water is able to keep a boat afloat.
4. Redraw the diagram above to show the block resting on its side. Calculate the pressure under the block when it is resting on its side.

Liquid pressure

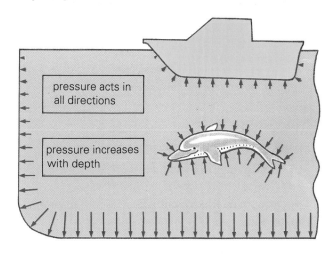

pressure acts in all directions

pressure increases with depth

The deeper you go into water, the greater the pressure becomes. This pressure pushes in all directions.

It is the pressure from water which keeps a boat afloat. Water pressing on the hull produces an upward push called an **upthrust**. This is strong enough to support the weight of the boat.

Car brakes use liquid pressure. When the brake pedal is pressed, a piston puts pressure on trapped brake fluid. The pressure is transmitted, through fluid in the pipes, to the wheels. There, the pressure pushes on pistons. These move the brake pads.

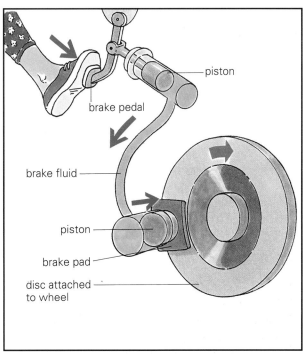

piston

brake pedal

brake fluid

piston

brake pad

disc attached to wheel

Turning forces

By the end of this spread, you should be able to:
- calculate the turning effect of a force
- explain why some things balance
- explain what makes things stable

Moments

Below, someone is using a spanner to turn a bolt. With a longer spanner, they could use the same force to produce an even greater turning effect.

The strength of a turning effect is called a **moment**. It can be calculated with this equation:

moment =	force ×	distance from turning point
in Nm	in N	in m

(The distance is the *shortest* distance from the turning point to the line of the force.)

Moments in balance

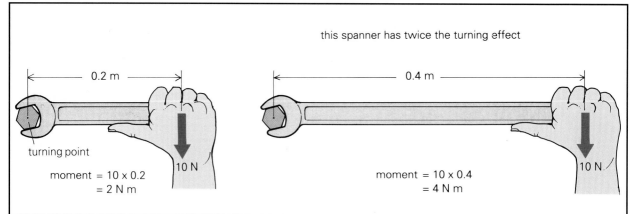

this spanner has twice the turning effect

0.2 m

turning point

moment = 10 × 0.2
       = 2 N m

10 N

0.4 m

moment = 10 × 0.4
       = 4 N m

10 N

Moments in balance

On the right, a plank has been balanced on a log. Different weights have been placed on both sides of the plank. They have been arranged so that the plank still balances.

The weight on the left has a turning effect to the left. The weight on the right has a turning effect to the right.

The two turning effects are equal. That is why the plank balances.

In other words, if something balances:

moment	=	moment
turning to the left		turning to the right

This is an example of the **law of moments**.

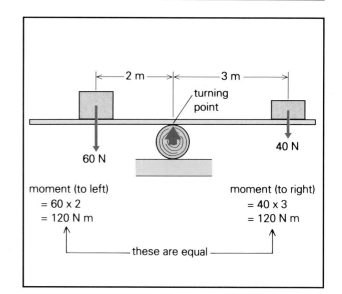

2 m   3 m

turning point

60 N   40 N

moment (to left)   moment (to right)
  = 60 × 2   = 40 × 3
  = 120 N m   = 120 N m

these are equal

Centre of mass

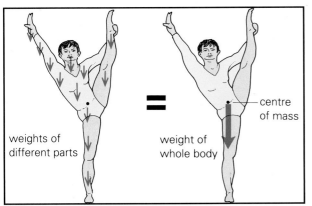

weights of different parts = weight of whole body

centre of mass

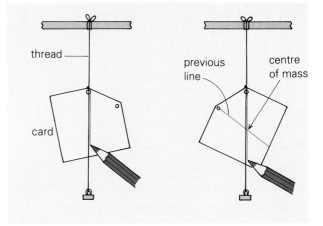

thread

card

previous line

centre of mass

Balancing on a beam is difficult. The secret lies in how you position your weight. All parts of the body have weight. Together, they act like a single force pulling at just one point. This point is called your **centre of mass** (or **centre of gravity**). To balance on a beam, you have to keep your centre of mass over the beam.

If you suspend a piece of card from some thread, it always hangs with its centre of mass in line with the thread. You can use this idea to find the centre of mass. Suspend the card from one corner and draw a vertical line on it. Do the same using another corner. Then see where the two lines cross.

Stability

If something is in a **stable** position, it will not topple over.

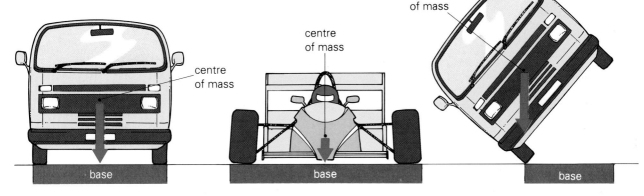

centre of mass

centre of mass

centre of mass

base

base

base

This van is in a stable position. If it starts to tip, its weight will pull it back again. As long as its centre of mass stays over its base, it will not topple.

This racing car is even more stable than the van. It has a lower centre of mass and a wider base. It has to be tipped much further before it starts to topple.

The van is now in an unstable position. Its centre of mass has just passed beyond the edge of its base. So its weight will pull it over.

The model crane on the right has a movable counterbalance.

1 Why does the crane need a counterbalance?
2 Why must the counterbalance be movable?
3 What is the moment of the 100 N force (about O)?
4 To balance the crane, what moment must the 400 N force have?
5 How far from O should the counterbalance be placed?
6 What is the maximum load the crane should lift?
7 Give *two* ways of making the design of the crane more stable.

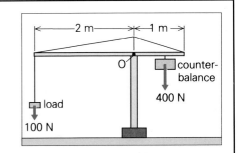

2 m — 1 m

O

counter-balance

400 N

load

100 N

Moving and stopping

By the end of this spread, you should be able to:
- calculate speed
- describe how friction is sometimes a nuisance and sometimes useful
- explain how speed affects road safety

Speed

Here is a simple method of measuring speed. You could use it to work out the speed of a cyclist:

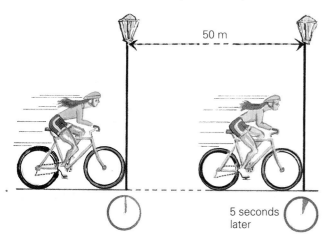

50 m

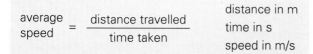

5 seconds later

Measure the distance between two points on a road, say two lamp posts. Measure the time taken to travel between these points. Then use this equation:

$$\text{average speed} = \frac{\text{distance travelled}}{\text{time taken}}$$

distance in m
time in s
speed in m/s

If the cyclist travels 50 metres in 5 seconds, her average speed is 50/5, which is 10 metres per second. This is written 10 m/s for short.

On most journeys, the speed changes, so the actual speed isn't always the same as the average speed. To find an actual speed, you have to find the distance travelled in the shortest time you can measure.

Friction

Friction is the force that tries to stop materials sliding past each other. There is friction between your hands when you rub them together. And there is friction between your shoes and the ground when you walk. **Air resistance** is also a type of friction. It slows you down when you ride a bike.

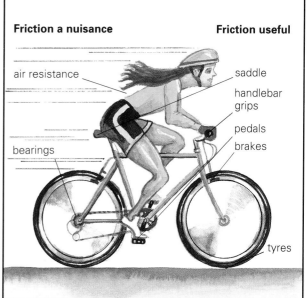

Friction a nuisance   **Friction useful**

air resistance   saddle
                                  handlebar grips
                                  pedals
bearings   brakes

                                  tyres

Using friction Friction can be useful. Without friction between the tyres and the ground, you would not be able to ride a bike. It would be like trying to ride on ice. You could not speed up, turn, or stop.

Brakes rely on friction. Cycles are slowed by rubber blocks pressed against the wheel rims. Cars are slowed by fibre pads pressed against discs attached to the wheels (for more on car brakes, see Spread 4.11).

Problems with friction Friction can also be a nuisance. Moving things are slowed by friction. Friction also produces heat. In machinery, grease and oil reduce friction so that moving parts do not overheat and seize up. Ball bearings and roller bearings reduce friction. Their rolling action means that a wheel does not have to rub against its shaft.

Speed and safety

In an emergency, the driver of a car may have to react quickly and apply the brakes.

The car's **stopping distance** depends on two things:
- The **thinking distance**. This is how far the car travels before the brakes are applied, while the driver is still reacting.
- The **braking distance**. This is how far the car then travels, after the brakes have been applied.

It takes an average driver about 0.6 seconds to react, and press the brake pedal. This is the driver's **reaction time**. During this time, the car does not slow down. And the higher its speed, the further it travels.

This is how to work out the thinking distance for a car travelling at 20 m/s (45 mph). The driver's reaction time is 0.6 seconds:

$$\text{speed} = \frac{\text{distance}}{\text{time}}$$

So, distance = speed × time

$$= 20 \times 0.6 = 12 \text{ metres}$$

So, the thinking distance is 12 metres

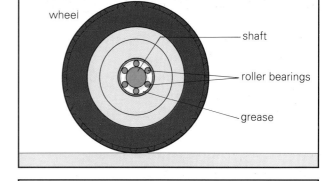

1 Mandy cycles 100 metres in 10 seconds. What is her average speed?
2 Look at the photograph on the opposite page. What features can you see for reducing friction?
3 For a car, where is friction a)*useful* b) a *nuisance*? Give *two* examples of each.
4 In the chart below, what is the thinking distance a) at 25 m/s b) at 30 m/s? Why does the thinking distance go up, even though the driver's reaction time stay the same?
5 Alcohol slows people's reactions. If a driver has a reaction time of 2 seconds a) what will his thinking distance be at 56 mph (25 m/s)? b) what will his stopping distance be? (You will need information from the chart to answer this.)

The chart shows the stopping distances for cars at different speeds. The figures are for a dry road. If the road is wet or icy, or the driver's reactions are slow, the stopping distances will be even greater.

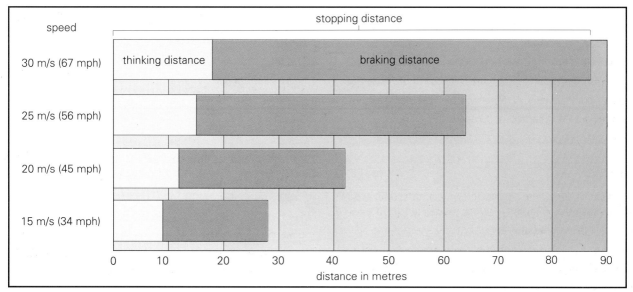

Machines, work, and power

By the end of this spread, you should be able to:
- explain how some machines magnify force, while others magnify movement
- calculate work and power

Machines help to make jobs easier. A machine can be something complicated like a car jack, or simple like a pair of scissors. The machines on this page have no motors. With each one, you put in a force. The machine puts out a force which does the job.

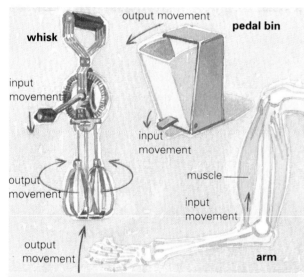

Movement magnifiers are machines which put out more movement than you put in. However, the output force is less than the input force.

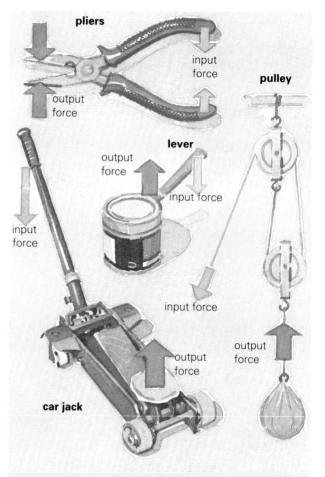

Force magnifiers are machines which put out more force than you put in. However, the output movement is less than the input movement.

Work

Scientists say that **work** is done whenever a force moves. Like energy, work is measured in **joules (J)**.

One joule of work is done when a force of 1 newton (N) moves a distance of 1 metre (m).

To calculate work, you can use this equation:

work done = force × distance
in J   in N   in m

For example, 6 joules of work are done when a force of 3 N moves a distance of 2 m.

There is a link between work and energy:
If, say, 6 joules of work are done, then 6 joules of energy are spent.

Inputs and outputs

The lever below is a force magnifier. The output force is *twice* the input force, but only moves *half* the distance. So the work output equals the work input:

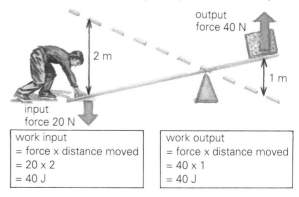

work input	work output
= force x distance moved	= force x distance moved
= 20 x 2	= 40 x 1
= 40 J	= 40 J

In the last example, the energy output is equal to the energy input. This means that the lever wastes no energy, so its **efficiency** is 100% (see spread 4.9 for more on efficiency).

Most machines waste energy because of friction in their moving parts. So their efficiency is less than 100%. This means that the energy output is *less* than the energy input. Note: the energy output can *never* be *more* than the energy input because that would break the law of conservation of energy (see Spread 4.7).

Power

If one engine has more **power** than another, it can do work at a faster rate.

Power is measured in **watts (W)**.

A power of 1 watt means that work is being done at the rate of 1 joule per second. Put another way, energy is being spent at the rate of 1 joule per second. So 1 W = 1 J/s.

A larger unit of power is the **kilowatt (kW)**. 1 kW = 1000 W. So a motor with a power output of 1 kW can do work at the rate of 1000 joules per second.

You can use these equations to calculate power:

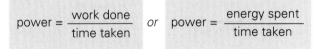

$$power = \frac{work\ done}{time\ taken} \quad or \quad power = \frac{energy\ spent}{time\ taken}$$

1. Give *three* examples of household machines which are force magnifiers.
2. Phil claims to have invented a machine which is both a force magnifier *and* a movement magnifier. Why would you not believe him?
3. If you use a force of 20 N to move a wheelbarrow 5 metres, how much work (in joules) do you do?
4. If, in question 3, it takes you 10 seconds to move the wheelbarrow, what is your power output?
5. If you lift a mass of 20 kg through a height of 4 metres in 8 seconds, what is your power output?

Typical power outputs

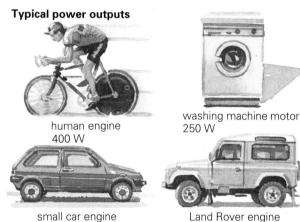

human engine
400 W

washing machine motor
250 W

small car engine
45 000 W

Land Rover engine
70 000 W

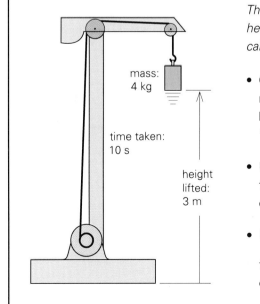

mass:
4 kg

time taken:
10 s

height
lifted:
3 m

The model crane on the left can lift a mass of 4 kg through a height of 3 metres in 10 seconds. This is how you would calculate its power output:

- Calculate the force being moved. (This is the weight being lifted. On Earth, it is 10 N for each kg of mass.)

  force (weight) = 4 × 10
  = 40 N

- Use *work = force x distance* to calculate the work output.

  work output = 40 × 3
  = 120 J

- Use *power* = $\frac{work\ done}{time\ taken}$ to calculate the power output.

  power output = $\frac{120}{10}$
  = 12 W

Sound waves

By the end of this spread, you should be able to:
- *explain what causes sound*
- *describe how sound travels as waves*
- *explain how echoes are produced*
- *describe how sounds can be absorbed*

Making sounds

When the cone of a loudspeaker vibrates, it stretches and squashes the air in front of it. The 'stretches' and 'squashes' travel outwards through the air as invisible waves. (In diagrams, the 'squashes' are often drawn as a series of lines.) When the waves enter your ear, you hear them as **sound**.

Sound waves spread through air just as ripples spread across water. However, sound waves make the air vibrate backwards and forwards, not up and down.

Sound needs a material to travel through

Sound waves can travel through solids and liquids, as well as gases. But they cannot travel through a vacuum (empty space). If there is nothing to stretch and squash, sound waves cannot be made.

Sound is caused by vibrations

The vibrations can be produced in different ways. You can see some examples below:

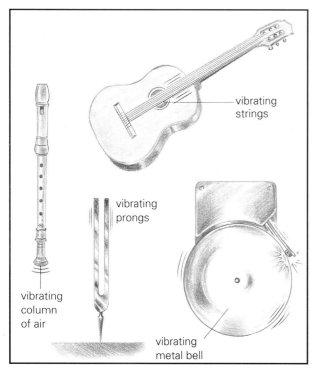

vibrating strings

vibrating prongs

vibrating column of air

vibrating metal bell

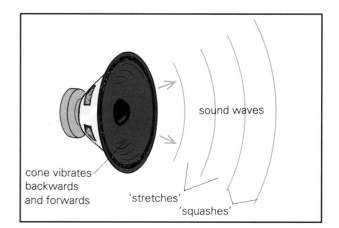

cone vibrates backwards and forwards

'stretches'

'squashes'

sound waves

The speed of sound

In air, the speed of sound is about 330 metres per second. The exact speed depends on the temperature.

Sound travels faster through water than it does through air, and even faster through most solids.

Sound is much slower than light, which travels at 300 000 *kilometres* per second. That is why you see a flash of lightning before you hear it. The light reaches you almost instantly.

Sound on screen

If you whistle into a microphone connected to a **cathode ray oscilloscope (CRO)**, a wavy line appears on the screen of the CRO. However, you aren't really seeing sound waves. The up-and-down line is a graph showing how the air next to the microphone vibrates backwards and forwards with time.

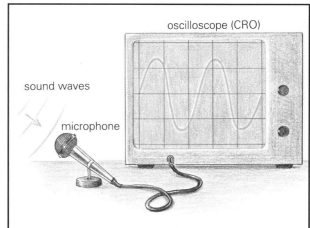

oscilloscope (CRO)

sound waves

microphone

Echoes

Hard surfaces, such as walls, reflect sound waves. When you hear an **echo**, you are hearing a reflected sound a short time after the original sound.

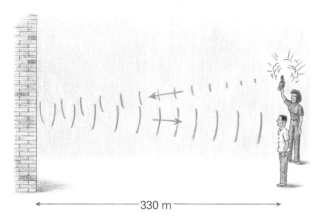

Finding the speed of sound You can use echoes to work out the speed of sound. The girl above is stood 330 metres from a wall. She fires a starting pistol. Her friend hears the echo 2 seconds later.

The sound has travelled a distance of 2 x 330 metres. The time taken is 2 seconds. So:

$$\text{speed of sound} = \frac{\text{distance travelled}}{\text{time taken}} = \frac{2 \times 330}{2}$$

$$= 330 \text{ m/s}$$

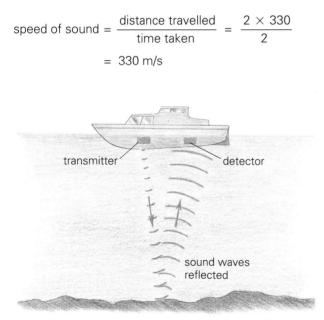

Echo-sounding Boats can use echo-sounding equipment to work out the depth of water beneath them. A sound pulse is sent down through the water. The time for the echo to return is measured. The longer the time, the deeper the water. A microchip can work out the depth and display it on a screen.

Absorbing sounds

Empty rooms sound echoey. The walls reflect the smallest sound, and it may take several seconds for the wave energy to be absorbed so that the sound dies away.

Echoes can be a nuisance in concert halls. Soft materials like carpets and curtains help to absorb sound waves, so do the clothes of the audience. Many large concert halls have specially-designed sound absorbers on the ceiling to make them less echoey.

The 'mushrooms' on the ceiling of this concert hall are sound absorbers to reduce unwanted echoes.

Assume that the speed of sound in air is 330 m/s.
1 Why cannot sound travel through a vacuum?
2 How could you show that sound travels in the form of waves?
3 Why do you hear lightning after you see it?
4 If you hear lightning 2 seconds after you see it, how far away is the lightning?
5 Chris shouts when he is 110 metres from a wall.
   a) What time does it take for the sound to reach the wall? b) When will Chris hear his echo?
6 What is *echo-sounding*? How does it work?
7 Why do some rooms sound echoey? What can be done to solve the problem?

Detecting sounds

By the end of this spread, you should be able to:
- describe how the ear works
- explain how hearing can be damaged
- describe how sounds can differ

The ear

Inside the ear, sound waves are detected and nerve impulses are sent to the brain for processing.

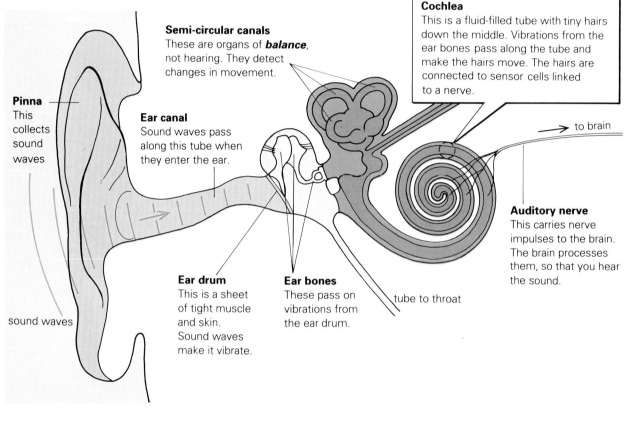

Semi-circular canals
These are organs of **balance**, not hearing. They detect changes in movement.

Pinna
This collects sound waves

Ear canal
Sound waves pass along this tube when they enter the ear.

sound waves

Ear drum
This is a sheet of tight muscle and skin. Sound waves make it vibrate.

Ear bones
These pass on vibrations from the ear drum.

tube to throat

hair

sensor cells

nerve (branch)

Cochlea
This is a fluid-filled tube with tiny hairs down the middle. Vibrations from the ear bones pass along the tube and make the hairs move. The hairs are connected to sensor cells linked to a nerve.

to brain

Auditory nerve
This carries nerve impulses to the brain. The brain processes them, so that you hear the sound.

Hearing problems

When sound waves enter the ear, the brain may not receive nerve impulses. Or the nerve impulses may be weak. Here are some of the problems that can cause deafness or poor hearing:
- The ear drum may be damaged.
- Bone growth may stop the ear bones moving.
- The cochlea or auditory nerve may be damaged.

The cochlea and auditory nerve can be damaged by very loud sounds. That is why you should not play a personal stereo at high volume. If you are exposed to loud sounds over a long period of time, the damage may be so gradual that you do not notice.

Noise

Unwanted sound is called **noise**. It can be annoying. It can also be damaging. Scientists check noise levels using meters marked in **decibels (dB)**.

	Noise level in dB
personal stereo, very loud	150
damage to ears	140
rock concert	110
some ear discomfort	90
telephone ringing	70
normal speech	60
whispering	40

Sounds different

Some sounds are louder than others. Some sounds are higher than others. To see how different sounds compare, you can use a microphone and CRO.

Amplitude and loudness The height of a peak or trough on the screen is called the **amplitude**. The higher the amplitude, the **louder** the sound will be.

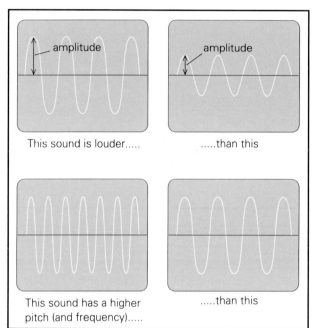

This sound is louder..... | .....than this

This sound has a higher pitch (and frequency)..... | .....than this

Frequency and pitch The **frequency** of a sound is the number of sound waves being sent out per second.

Frequency is measured in **hertz (Hz)**. If a sound has a frequency of, say, 100 Hz, then 100 sound waves are being sent out every second.

The higher the frequency, the higher the note sounds. Musicians say that it has a higher **pitch**.

If the frequency increases, you see more waves on the CRO screen. The peaks of the waves are closer together.

1 In the ear, what job is done by a) the ear drum b) the ear bones c) the cochlea?
2 Explain why a personal stereo played at high volume can damage your hearing.
3 A sound has a *frequency* of *200 Hz*. What does this tell you about the sound waves?
4 What difference will you hear in a sound if there is an increase in a) amplitude b) frequency?
5 In hospitals, why are sound waves sometimes used instead of X-rays? What are the sound waves used for?

Seeing with sound

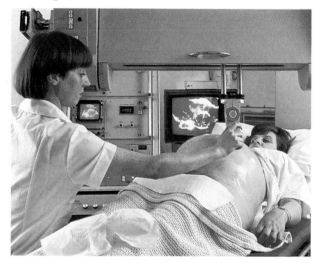

Sounds which are too high for the human ear to hear are called **ultrasonic sounds**, or **ultrasound**. Ultrasound can be used to check an unborn baby in the womb, as above. An ultrasound transmitter is moved over the mother's body. A detector picks up sound waves reflected from different layers inside the body. The signals are processed by a computer, which puts an image on a screen. The method is safer than using X-rays because X-rays damage body cells.

low frequency					high frequency
20 Hz	100 Hz	1 000 Hz	10 000 Hz	20 000 Hz	ultrasonic sounds
drum	low note from singer	high note from singer	whistle	highest note heard by human ear	
low pitch					high pitch

Rays of light

By the end of this spread, you should be able to:
* *explain how light can be reflected and refracted*

Light is radiation which your eyes can detect. It normally travels in straight lines. In diagrams, lines called **rays** show which way the light is going.

You see some things because they give off their own light: the Sun or a light bulb for example.

You see other things because daylight, or other light, bounces off them. They **reflect** light, and some goes into your eyes. That is why you can see this page.

The white parts of the page reflect light well, so they look bright. However, the black letters **absorb** most of the light striking them. They reflect very little. That is why they look so dark.

Transparent materials, like glass, let light pass through them. They **transmit** light.

Reflection and mirrors

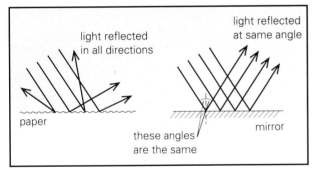

light reflected in all directions

light reflected at same angle

paper

these angles are the same

mirror

Most surfaces are uneven, or contain materials which scatter light. The light bounces off them in all directions. However, mirrors are smooth and shiny. They reflect light in a regular way.

In the diagram at the top on the right, light from a bulb is being reflected by a mirror. Some is reflected into the girl's eye. To the girl, the light seems to come from a point behind the mirror. She sees an **image** of the bulb in that position.

The image is the same size as the original bulb, and the same distance from the mirror. However its left and right sides are the wrong way round. It is **laterally inverted**, just like these letters:

ꓤOꓤꓤIM A NI SIHT ƎꓘIꓳ SꓘOOꓳ ⅁NITIꓤW

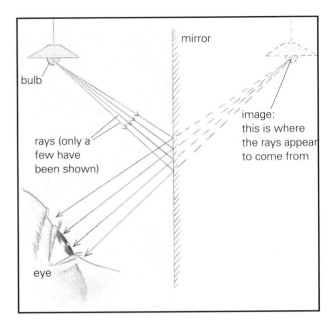

mirror

bulb

rays (only a few have been shown)

image: this is where the rays appear to come from

eye

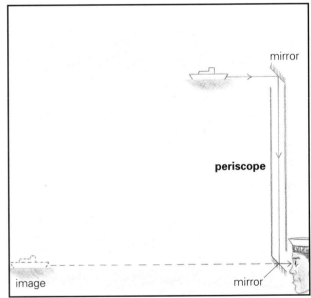

mirror

periscope

image

mirror

Periscope A periscope uses two mirrors to give you a higher view than normal. The image you see is the right way round because one mirror cancels out the lateral inversion of the other.

1 Hot, glowing things give off light. How can this page give off light if it isn't hot and glowing?
2 A wall reflects light. So does a mirror. What difference is there in the way they reflect light?
3 Why does a periscope need two mirrors?

Refraction

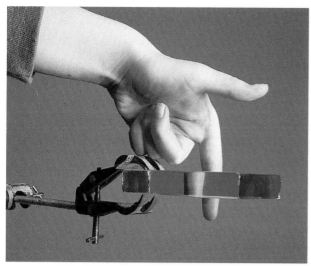

The light passing through the glass block above has been bent. The bending is called **refraction**: It happens with other transparent materials as well as glass.

Below, you can see how scientists explain refraction. Light is made up of tiny waves (see spread 4.19). These travel more slowly in glass than in air. One side of the light beam is slowed before the other. This makes the light waves bend.

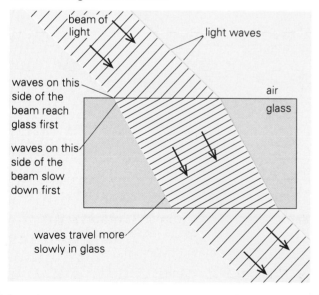

beam of light
light waves
waves on this side of the beam reach glass first
waves on this side of the beam slow down first
air
glass
waves travel more slowly in glass

4 What is *refraction*? Give an example.
5 Why does a beam of light bend when it enters glass at an angle? Why does it *not* bend if it enters the glass 'square on'.
6 What is an *optical fibre*? How does it work?

Reflection and fibres

The inside face of a glass block can act as a perfect mirror - provided light strikes it at a shallow enough angle. No light is refracted. All is reflected. Scientists call this **total internal reflection**.

Total internal reflection is used in **optical fibres**. These are thin, flexible strands of glass or plastic. When light enters one end of a fibre, it is reflected from side to side, until it comes out of the other end. (High-quality fibres have an outer layer of glass or plastic to protect the core which carries the light.)

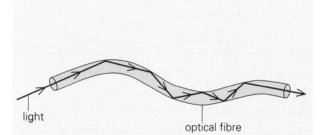

light
optical fibre

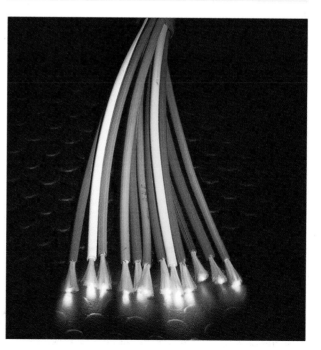

Optical fibres are used to carry telephone calls. Sound waves 'pulsate' the light from a tiny laser at one end of the fibre. At the other end, the light pulsations are detected and changed into electrical signals. These make the telephone give out sound.

4·18 Lenses at work

By the end of this spread, you should be able to:
- *describe what different lenses do to light*
- *describe some uses of convex lenses*
- *explain how spectacles work*

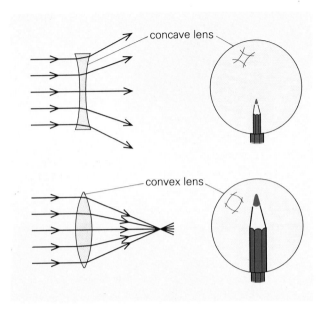

Lenses bend light and form images. There are two main types of lens:

Concave lenses these are thin in the middle and thickest round the edge. They bend light outwards. Looking through a concave lens makes things appear smaller.

Convex lenses these are thickest in the middle and thin round the edge. They bend light inwards. A convex lens makes *very close* things look bigger. Used in this way, the lens is often called a **magnifying glass**.

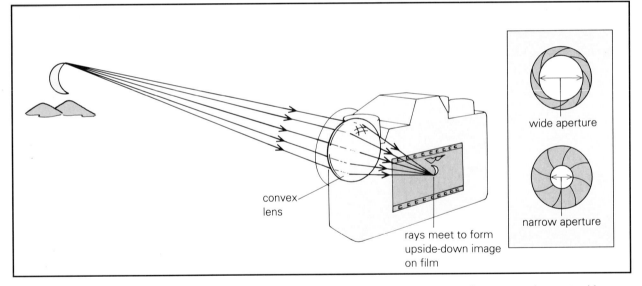

convex lens

rays meet to form upside-down image on film

wide aperture

narrow aperture

With *distant* things, a convex lens brings rays to a focus. The rays form a small, upside-down image which you can pick up on a screen. It is called a **real image** because the rays actually meet to produce it. (The image you see in a flat mirror isn't formed by rays meeting. It is called a **virtual image**.)

If a distant thing moves closer to a convex lens, the image moves further away. It also gets bigger. This idea is used in a **projector**. A brightly-lit piece of film is put fairly close to a convex lens. The result is a large, real image on a screen many metres away. For an upright image, the film must be upside-down.

A **camera** uses a convex lens to produce a real image. The image is formed on the **film** at the back. The film is coated with light-sensitive chemicals. These are changed by the different shades and colours of light. But they must only be exposed to light for a very short time. That is why a camera needs a **shutter** which opens and shuts very quickly.

To focus on things at different distances, the lens is moved in or out. This changes its distance from the film. Behind the lens, metals plates can alter the size of the **aperture** (hole) through which the light passes. A bigger aperture lets in more light.

The eye

Like a camera, the human eye uses a convex lens system to form a tiny, real, image at the back. The image is upside-down. However, the brain gets so used to this that it thinks the image is the right way up!

For focusing on things at different distances, tiny muscles make the eye lens thinner or fatter. However, many people can still not get a clearly-focused image. So they have to wear spectacles (or contact lenses) to help their eye lenses.

Lens
This is made thicker or thinner to adjust the focus.

Cornea
This and the watery liquid behind it bend the light inwards.

Pupil
Light enters the eye through this hole, which looks black.

Iris
This is usually brown or blue. It changes size to make the pupil bigger or smaller. In a dark room, the pupil is made bigger to let in more light.

Retina
This is where the image is formed. It contains millions of light-sensitive cells which send out nerve impulses when they receive light.

clear jelly

Optic nerve
This carries nerve impulses to the brain, where they are processed.

Short sight In a short-sighted eye, the eye lens cannot become thin enough for looking at distant things. So the rays are bent inwards too much. They meet before the reach the retina.

Long sight In a long-sighted eye, the eye lens cannot become thick enough for looking at close things. So the rays are not bent inwards enough. When they reach the retina, they have still not met.

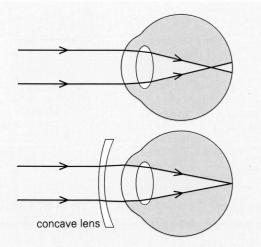

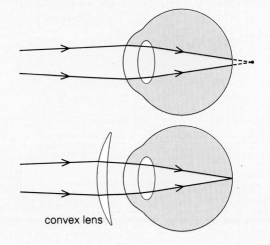

A *concave* spectacle lens solves the problem. It bends the rays outwards a little before they enter the eye.

A *convex* spectacle lens solves the problem. It bends the rays inwards a little before they enter the eye.

---

1 How would a paper clip look if you saw it through a) a concave lens b) a convex lens? (Assume the paper clip is close to the lens.)

2 Name *three* things which make use of a convex lens. What job does the lens do in each one?

3 Give *three* ways in which the human eye is similar to a camera.

4 What is the difference between a short-sighted eye and a normal eye? What type of spectacle lens does a short-sighted person need? Why?

Across the spectrum

By the end of this spread, you should be able to:
- explain how a prism forms a spectrum
- describe the different types of electromagnetic waves, and what they are used for

Forming a spectrum

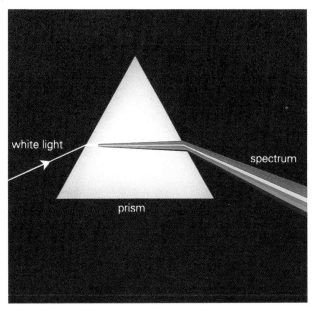

white light

spectrum

prism

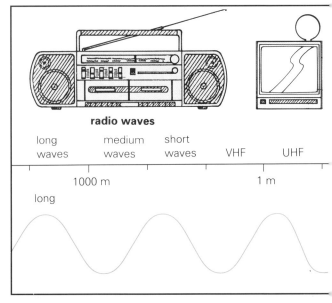

radio waves

long waves	medium waves	short waves	VHF	UHF

1000 m   1 m

long

A narrow beam of white light enters a triangular glass block called a **prism**. The light is refracted (bent) as it goes into the prism, and again as it comes out. The refracted light spreads slightly to form a range of colours called a **spectrum**.

Most people think they can see six colours in the spectrum: red, orange, yellow, green, blue, and violet. But really, there is a continuous change of colour from one end to the other.

How scientists think the spectrum is formed

White is not a single colour, but a mixture of colours. A prism splits them up.

Light is made up of tiny waves. These have different **wavelengths**. The eyes and brain sense different wavelengths as different colours. Red waves are the longest and violet the shortest.

When light enters glass, it slows down and bends (see Spread 4.17). Waves of violet light slow down more than waves of red light. So they are bent more. That is why the different colours are spread out. The spreading effect is called **dispersion**.

Raindrops act like tiny prisms and split sunlight into its different colours.

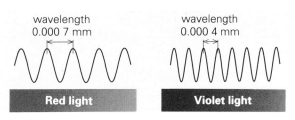

wavelength 0.000 7 mm

wavelength 0.000 4 mm

Red light   **Violet light**

The electromagnetic spectrum

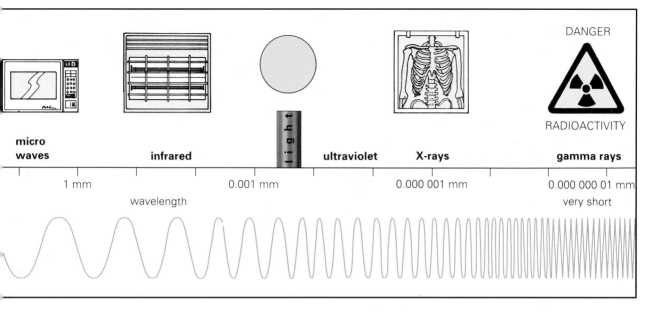

| micro waves | infrared | light | ultraviolet | X-rays | gamma rays |

DANGER
RADIOACTIVITY

1 mm   0.001 mm   0.000 001 mm   0.000 000 01 mm

wavelength   very short

Beyond the colours of the spectrum, there are types of radiation which the eye cannot see. Light is just one member of a much larger family of waves called the ***electromagnetic spectrum***.

Electromagnetic waves have these things in common:
- They are electric and magnetic ripples, given off when electrons or other charged particles vibrate or lose energy.
- They can travel though empty space.
- Their speed through space is 300 000 km/s.

Radio waves These are produced by making electrons vibrate in an aerial. They cannot be seen or heard. But they can be sent out in a pattern which tells a radio or TV what sounds or pictures to make.

Microwaves These are similar to radio waves, but of shorter wavelength. They are used for radar, for satellite communication, and for beaming telephone and TV signals around the country.

Some microwaves are absorbed by food. This makes the food hot. The idea is used in microwave ovens.

Infrared Hot things like fires and radiators all give off infrared radiation. In fact, everything gives off some infrared. If you absorb it, it heats you up.

Light This is the visible part of the spectrum - the part which the eye can detect.

Ultraviolet The eye cannot detect ultraviolet, but there is lots of it in sunlight. This is the type of radiation which gives you a sun tan. Too much can damage your eyes and skin.

Fluorescent 'day glo' paints and inks absorb the ultraviolet in sunlight and change its energy into visible light. That is why they glow so brightly.

X-rays Shorter wavelengths can penetrate dense metals. Longer wavelengths can pass through flesh, but not bone. So they can be used to take 'shadow' photographs of bones. Only brief bursts of X-rays must be used for this. X-rays are very dangerous and damage living cells deep in the body.

Gamma rays These are given off by radioactive materials (see Spread 3.9). They have the same effects as X-rays and are very dangerous.

1 Which is refracted most by a prism, red light or violet light? Explain why.
The following questions are about these waves:
gamma radio micro X-rays light ultraviolet infrared
2 Put the waves in order of wavelength, starting with the longest wavelength.
3 Which of the waves a) can be detected by the eye b) are used for communications c) are used in cooking d) can pass through flesh e) can damage cells deep in the body?

Sun, Earth, and Moon

By the end of this spread, you should be able to:
- explain why the Earth has seasons
- explain why the Moon has phases
- describe some of the effects of gravity
- describe some of the uses of satellites

The Sun

The Sun is a huge, hot, brightly glowing ball of gas, called a **star**. It is 150 000 000 kilometres away from us. Its diameter, 1.4 million kilometres, is more than a hundred times that of the Earth. The Sun is extremely hot: 6000 ºC on the surface, rising to 15 000 000 ºC in the centre. The heat comes from nuclear reactions deep in its core.

Earth, orbiting and spinning

The Earth moves round the Sun in a path called an **orbit**. One orbit takes just over 365 days, which is the length of our year. As it moves through space, the Earth spins slowly on its axis once a day. This gives us day and night as we move from the sunny side facing the Sun to the dark side away from it.

The Earth's axis is tilted by 23.5º. This means that in Britain, for example, the Sun seems to climb higher in the sky in June than it does in December. Also, there are more hours of daylight in June than there are in December. That is why there are different seasons.

When you look at the moon, some of it is usually in shadow. You only see the sunlit part.

A view of the Moon

The Moon is in orbit around the Earth, and 380 000 kilometres away from us. It is smaller than the Earth, and has a rocky, cratered surface. We only see the Moon because its surface reflects sunlight.

The Moon orbits the Earth once every 27 days. It also spins on its axis once every 27 days. That is why it always keeps the same face toward us.

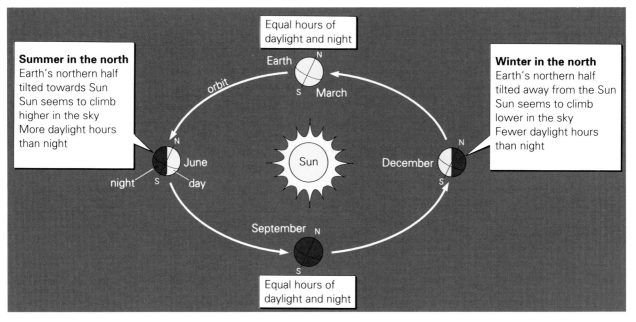

Summer in the north
Earth's northern half tilted towards Sun
Sun seems to climb higher in the sky
More daylight hours than night

Winter in the north
Earth's northern half tilted away from the Sun
Sun seems to climb lower in the sky
Fewer daylight hours than night

Equal hours of daylight and night

Earth

March

orbit

June

night   day

Sun

December

September

Equal hours of daylight and night

As the Moon orbits the Earth, we see different amounts of its surface depending on the position of the Sun. Sometimes we see the whole face (a Full Moon). Sometimes we see less than half the face (a crescent Moon), because the rest is in shadow. And sometimes we saw almost no face (a New Moon). These different views of the Moon are called **phases**. A complete sequence of phases takes 29.5 days, and not 27. That is because the Earth also changes position as it slowly orbits the Sun.

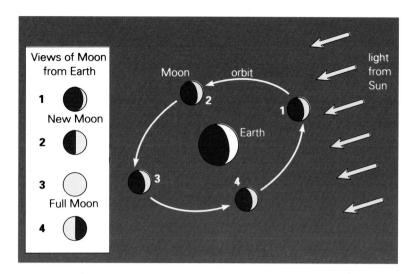

Gravity in action

We are pulled to the Earth by the force of gravity. No one knows what causes gravity. But scientists know that there is a gravitational pull between *all* masses:

- small masses have a weaker pull than large masses
- distant masses have a weaker pull than close masses.

The pull between everyday things is far too weak to detect. It only becomes strong if one of the things has a huge mass, like the Earth.

The gravitational force between the Earth and the Sun holds the Earth in orbit around the Sun. The gravitational force between the Moon and the Earth holds the Moon in orbit around the Earth.

Satellites in orbit

There are hundreds of satellites in orbit around the Earth. Some carry cameras for surveying the Earth's surface. Some have telescopes for observing distant stars. Telescopes in space can pick up light or other radiation before it is disturbed by the Earth's atmosphere. Some satellites give out navigation signals. And some are used for communications. They relay TV pictures and telephone messages between different places on Earth.

Communications and navigation satellites are normally in **geostationary** orbits. This means that the orbit has been carefully chosen so that the satellite orbits at the same rate as the Earth turns. From the ground, the satellite appears to be in a fixed position in the sky.

1. How long does it take for a) the Moon to orbit the Earth? b) the Earth to orbit the Sun?
2. In the north, why does the Sun seem to climb higher in the sky in June than in December?
3. Why do we always see the same side of the Moon?
4. We can see the Sun because it is glowing. How are we able to see the Moon?
5. Why do we sometimes see the Moon as a crescent rather than a full disc?
6. If the Moon and Earth were further apart, how would this affect the gravitational pull between them?
7. Communications satellites are in orbit, and moving. Yet satellites dishes on the ground point in a fixed direction. How is this is possible?

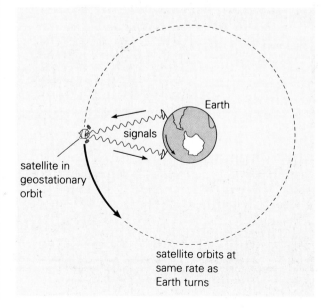

satellite orbits at same rate as Earth turns

Planets, stars, and galaxies

By the end of this spread, you should be able to:
* *explain what the Solar System is, and its place in the Universe.*

The Solar System

The Earth is one of many **planets** in orbit around the Sun. The Sun, planets, and other objects in orbit, are together known as the **Solar System**.

Planets are not hot enough to give off their own light. We can only see them because they reflect the Sun's light. From Earth, they look like tiny dots in the night sky. Without a telescope, it is difficult to tell whether you are looking at a star or a planet.

Most of the planets move in near-circular orbits around the Sun. Many have smaller **moons** in orbit around them.

Comets are collections of ice, gas, and dust which orbit the Sun and reflect its light. They have highly elliptical orbits which bring them close to the Sun and then far out in the Solar System.

Saturn is a gassy giant. Its 'rings' are billions of orbiting bits of ice which reflect light.

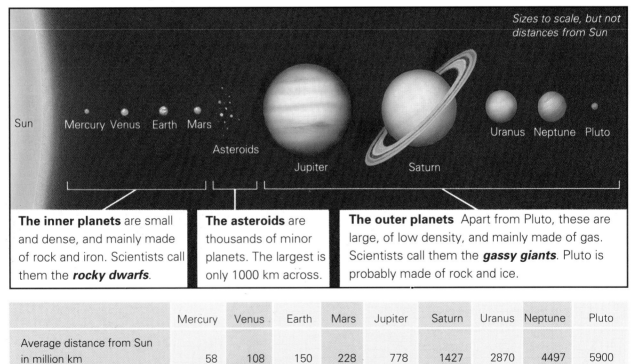

Sizes to scale, but not distances from Sun

Sun Mercury Venus Earth Mars Asteroids Jupiter Saturn Uranus Neptune Pluto

The inner planets are small and dense, and mainly made of rock and iron. Scientists call them the **rocky dwarfs**.

The asteroids are thousands of minor planets. The largest is only 1000 km across.

The outer planets Apart from Pluto, these are large, of low density, and mainly made of gas. Scientists call them the **gassy giants**. Pluto is probably made of rock and ice.

	Mercury	Venus	Earth	Mars	Jupiter	Saturn	Uranus	Neptune	Pluto
Average distance from Sun in million km	58	108	150	228	778	1427	2870	4497	5900
Time for one orbit in years	0.24	0.62	1	1.88	11.86	29.46	84.01	164.8	247
Diameter in km	4900	12 100	12 800	6800	143 000	120 000	51 000	49 000	3900
Average surface temperature	350 °C	480 °C	22 °C	-23 °C	-150 °C	-180 °C	-210 °C	-220 °C	-230 °C
Number of moons	0	0	1	2	16	23	15	8	1

Stars and galaxies

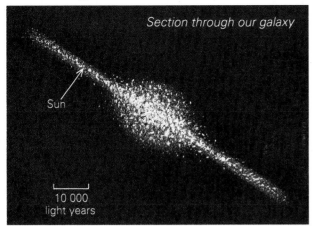

Section through our galaxy

Sun

10 000
light years

Our Sun is just one star in a huge star system called a *galaxy*. This contains over 100 billion stars. It is so big that a beam of light, travelling at 300 000 kilometres *per second*, would take 100 000 years to cross it! Scientists say that the galaxy is 100 000 **light years** across.

Ours is not the only galaxy. In the whole **Universe**, there are over 100 billion galaxies.

Our galaxy is called the **Milky Way**. You can see the edge of its disc as a bright band of stars across the night sky. The Milky Way is a member of a local cluster of about 30 galaxies. The other major member is the **Andromeda Galaxy**.

Exploring space

People have stood on the Moon, unmanned spacecraft have landed on Mars and Venus, and space probes have passed close to most of the outer planets. But travelling further into space is a problem. The *Voyager 2* probe took 12 years to reach Neptune. At that speed, it would take over 100 000 years to reach the nearest star! To find out more about stars and galaxies, we have to rely on the light and other forms of radiation picked up by telescopes.

The Andromeda Galaxy is 2 million light years away.

Models of the Universe

Scientists create descriptions called **models** to explain what they observe. Over the centuries, various models of the Universe have been proposed (put forward). The models have been improved as new instruments have given better observations.

Century	
2nd BC	**Ptolemy** proposes that the Earth is a sphere at the centre of the Universe. The Sun, Moon, planets, and stars move around it.
16th	**Copernicus** proposes that the Sun is at the centre of the Universe, with the Earth and planets moving around it.
18th	**Herschel** proposes that the Sun is in a huge, disc-shaped galaxy of stars.
20th	**Hubble** proposes that our galaxy is just one of billions, and that the Universe is expanding.

1 Which is the largest planet in the Solar System?
2 Which planets are smaller than the Earth?
3 Which planets are colder than the Earth? Why?
4 Name the planets known as *gassy giants*.
5 Why do planets give off light?
6 What link can you see between the time for a planet's orbit and its distance from the Sun?

7 Carbon dioxide in Venus' atmosphere produces a greenhouse effect (global warming). What clues are there for this in the table on the left?
8 What is a) *galaxy* b) a *light year*?
9 What other large galaxy belongs to the same cluster as our own? How long does its light take to reach us? Why are humans unlikely to visit it?

Summary

The spread number in brackets tells you where to find more information.

- Animals and plants feed, respire, excrete, grow, move, reproduce, show sensitivity, and are made of cells. *(2.1)*

- Plant cells absorb the Sun's energy. They use it to make their own food from simple substances. This process is called photosynthesis. *(2.2)*

- Plant and animal cells get energy by combining food with oxygen. This process is called respiration. *(2.2)*

- Insects or the wind can carry pollen from one flower to another. Pollen contains male sex cells which can fertilize female sex cells. Fertilized cells become seeds, which are scattered. *(2.3)*

- The skeleton supports the body, protects internal organs, and has joints for movement. Joints are moved by pairs of muscles. *(2.4)*

- The body is controlled by the central nervous system (brain and spinal cord). *(2.4)*

- As food passes along the gut, it is digested and then absorbed into the blood. *(2.5)*

- Food contains five main types of nutrient: carbohydrates, fats, proteins, minerals, and vitamins. *(2.5)*

- Blood carries oxygen, digested food, water, waste products, heat, and hormones. It also carries antibodies, which are used to fight disease. *(2.6)*

- The heart is really two pumps. One circulates blood through the lungs. The other circulates blood round the rest of the body. *(2.6)*

- In the lungs, oxygen passes into the blood, and carbon dioxide and water are removed. *(2.7)*

- One of the liver's jobs is to keep the blood topped up with the right amount of 'fuel' (glucose). *(2.7)*

- The kidneys filter unwanted substances from the blood. These pass out of the body as urine. *(2.7)*

- A woman's ovaries release an ovum about once every 28 days. If the ovum is fertilized by a sperm from a man, it may embed itself in the uterus wall and develop into an embryo. If not, the uterus lining will break up and pass out of the woman when she has her period. *(2.8)*

- In the uterus, a developing baby gets food and oxygen from its mother's blood through the placenta and umbilical cord. *(2.9)*

- Things which affect the mother's blood, such as smoking and disease, can also affect the baby. *(2.9)*

- Microbes which cause disease are known as germs. They can be transferred by air, contact, animals, and contaminated food. *(2.10)*

- Defending against disease is the job of your immune system. The defenders are the white blood cells. *(2.10)*

- Some microbes make food rot. Methods of slowing the process include pasteurizing, canning, drying, and refrigerating. *(2.11)*

- Some microbes are useful. They are used in making bread, cheese, and alcohol. *(2.11)*

- Animals with backbones are called vertebrates. The five main groups of vertebrates are fish, amphibians, reptiles, birds, and mammals. *(2.12)*

- Some of your characteristics you inherit. Others depend on your environment. *(2.13)*

- The chemical instructions for your inherited characteristics are called genes. Genes are small sections of the chromosomes in your cells. *(2.13)*

- By selecting the parents carefully, animals and plants can be bred to give the characteristics that breeders want. *(2.13)*

- Animals and plants are affected by non-living and living factors in their environment. Conditions can change daily or seasonally, and habitats may be shared with other organisms. These factors affect population sizes. *(2.14)*

- Humans grow crops, take materials from the ground, and burn fuels. These activities affect other populations of animals and plants, and are often a cause of pollution. *(2.15)*

- Plants are food for animals, which are food for other animals, and so on, in a food chain. Energy is lost from the chain at every stage. *(2.16)*

- Decomposers are microbes which feed on the remains of dead plants and animals. They put useful chemicals back into the soil. *(2.16)*

- Living things are made of atoms. Carbon and nitrogen are two types of atom which are recycled by living things. *(2.17)*

Summary

The spread number in brackets tells you where to find more information.

- Materials can be solid, liquid, or gas. *(3.1)*

- Density can be measured in kg/m³:

$$\text{density} = \frac{\text{mass}}{\text{volume}} \qquad (3.1)$$

- Metals, ceramics, plastics, glasses, and fibres are groups of materials with different properties. *(3.1)*

- Everything on Earth is made from about 90 simple substances called elements. Atoms of different elements can join together in chemical reactions to form new substances called compounds. *(3.2)*

- The reactivity series tells you how reactive metals are compared with each other. *(3.2)*

- If one substance (the solute) dissolves in another (the solvent), the result is a solution. *(3.3)*

- All acids contain hydrogen. If an acid reacts with a metal, hydrogen gas is given off. *(3.4)*

- A base will neutralize an acid. The result is a solution containing a salt. *(3.4)*

- Acids turn litmus red, alkalis turn it blue. *(3.4)*

- The strength of an acid or alkali is measured on the pH scale. pH1 is a very strong acid, pH14 is a very strong alkali, pH7 is neutral. *(3.4)*

- In the periodic table, elements in the same column have similar properties and similar arrangements of outer shell electrons. *(3.5)*

- Solids, liquids, and gases are made up of tiny particles which are constantly on the move. *(3.6)*

- For a fixed mass of gas, if the pressure *(P)*, volume *(V)* or Kelvin temperature *(T)* change, then:

$$\frac{P_1 \times V_1}{T_1} = \frac{P_2 \times V_2}{T_2} \qquad (3.7)$$

- Atoms have a nucleus of protons (+ charge) and neutrons (no charge), with electrons (– charge) moving around it. *(3.8)*

- Some atoms bond together by sharing electrons. This is called covalent bonding. A molecule is a group of atoms joined by covalent bonds. *(3.8)*

- Charged atoms are called ions. They are atoms which have gained or lost electrons. *(3.8)*

- Radioactive materials give out nuclear radiation. The main types of nuclear radiation are alpha particles, beta particles, and gamma rays (waves). *(3.9)*

- Some chemicals reactions are exothermic: they give out energy (heat). Others are endothermic: they take in energy. *(3.10)*

- The rate of a reaction depends on the size of the bits, concentration, temperature, and presence of a catalyst. *(3.10)*

- When an element burns, it combines with oxygen and an oxide is produced. *(3.11)*

- Most fuels are compounds of hydrogen and carbon. When they burn, the main products are carbon dioxide and water. *(3.11)*

- Three things are needed for combustion (burning): fuel, oxygen, and heat. *(3.11)*

- If a metal's surface becomes oxidized, the result is called corrosion. *(3.11)*

- The more reactive a metal, the more difficult it is to separate from its ore. Iron is separated from its ore by smelting. But electrolysis is needed to produce aluminium. *(3.12)*

- Common salt (sodium chloride) is an important source of other chemicals, including chlorine and sodium hydroxide. *(3.13)*

- Limestone is used to make cement and concrete. It is also needed for steel-making. *(3.13)*

- The fractions (parts) of crude oil can be separated by distillation. Some are used as fuels. Others are used in making plastics. *(3.14)*

- Air is a mixture of gases. It is mainly nitrogen (78%) and oxygen (21%). *(3.14)*

- Some places are hotter than others. This sets up pressure differences in the atmosphere. Pressure differences cause winds. *(3.15)*

- Clouds, rain, and dew are the result of water vapour cooling and condensing. *(3.15)*

- On Earth, water evaporates, condenses to form clouds, and then falls as rain. This is called the water cycle. *(3.16)*

- Rock can be weakened by the weather, broken into bits, eroded, transported, and then deposited. Eventually, it can form part of new rock. This process is called the rock cycle. *(3.16)*

- There are three main types of rock: igneous, sedimentary, and metamorphic. *(3.17)*

Summary

The spread number in brackets tells you where to find more information.

- A current is a flow of electrons. *(4.1)*
- Metals and carbon are good conductors of electricity. Most nonmetals are insulators. *(4.1)*
- Like charges repel. Unlike charges attract. *(4.1)*
- For a current to flow, a circuit must be unbroken. *(4.1)*
- Current is measured in amperes (A). Voltage is measured in volts (V). *(4.2)*
- Bulbs (or other components) can be connected in series or in parallel. *(4.2)*
- Some conductors have more resistance than others. When a current flows through a resistance, energy is given off as heat. This effect is used in heating elements. *(4.3)*
- 1 kW h is the energy supplied to a 1 kilowatt appliance in 1 hour. *(4.3)*
- Circuits can be controlled by logic gates, such as AND, OR, and NOT gates. The possible input and output settings are given in truth tables. *(4.4)*
- Like poles of a magnet repel, unlike poles attract. *(4.5)*
- Electromagnets are used in relays, circuit breakers, and loudspeakers. *(4.5)*
- Electric motors use a current and magnetism to produce motion. Generators use motion and magnetism to produce a current. *(4.6)*
- Transformers step AC voltages up or down. *(4.6)*
- Energy can be measured in joules (J). *(4.7)*
- Energy can change into different forms, but it cannot be made or destroyed. This is called the law of conservation of energy. *(4.7)*
- Heat can travel by conduction, convection, or radiation. *(4.8)*
- Fuels like coal, oil, and natural gas are non-renewable. Energy sources like the wind, and water behind dams, are renewable. *(4.9)*
- If an engine has an efficiency of 30%, then 30% of its fuel's energy is changed into movement energy. The rest is wasted as heat. *(4.9)*
- In one way or another, nearly all of our energy originally came from the Sun. *(4.10)*
- Force is measured in newtons (N). *(4.11)*
- Pressure $= \dfrac{\text{force}}{\text{area}}$ *(4.11)*

- Moment = force x distance from turning point. If something is balanced, the total left-turning moment is equal to the total right-turning moment. This is the law of moments. *(4.12)*
- Average speed $= \dfrac{\text{distance travelled}}{\text{time taken}}$ *(4.13)*
- The force of friction provides grip. But in machinery, it wastes energy. *(4.13)*
- Some machines are force magnifiers, others are movement magnifiers. *(4.14)*
- Work, like energy, can be measured in joules (J): Work done = force x distance moved *(4.14)*
- Power can be measured in watts (W): Power $= \dfrac{\text{work done}}{\text{time taken}}$ or $\dfrac{\text{energy spent}}{\text{time taken}}$ *(4.14)*
- Sound is caused by vibrations. *(4.15)*
- Sound waves can travel through solids, liquids, and gases, but not through a vacuum. *(4.15)*
- Echoes are reflected sounds which you hear a short time after the original sound. *(4.15)*
- Sound vibrations are detected by sensor cells in the ear. The higher the amplitude, the louder the sound. The higher the frequency, the higher the pitch. *(4.16)*
- You see this page because it reflects light. A mirror reflects light in a regular way. *(4.17)*
- Light bends when it enters glass or water. This is called refraction. *(4.17)*
- Convex lenses are used in the eye, camera, and projector to form images. *(4.18)*
- White light is a mixture of all the colours of the rainbow. *(4.19)*
- The electromagnetic spectrum is made up of radio waves, microwaves, infrared, light, ultraviolet, X-rays, and gamma rays. *(4.19)*
- The Earth orbits the Sun, held by the force of gravity. The Moon orbits the Earth. *(4.20)*
- We see the Moon because it reflects the Sun's light. But part of the Moon is often in shadow. *(4.20)*
- The Solar System is mainly made up of the Sun and its planets. The Sun is one star in a vast galaxy of 100 billion stars. There are more than 100 billion galaxies in the whole Universe. *(4.21)*

Answers to questions on spreads

2.1
1 Living things feed, respire, excrete, grow, move, reproduce, show sensitivity, are made of cells 2 Plants make own food, animals move to find food; cells different (see 5) 3 Plants growing towards light 4 Both have a nucleus, cytoplasm, and cell membrane 5 Plant cells have cellulose wall, chloroplasts, cell sap 6 Contain chlorophyll which absorbs energy in sunlight 7 Control centre of cell 8 Releasing energy from food; takes place in cells 9 Group of similar cells; organ

2.2
1 a) Carbon dioxide b) Oxygen 2 Sugar 3 No light 4 Healthy growth (making body proteins) 5 Stoma 6 Stream of water (and dissolved minerals) moving up through plant 7 a) Oxygen b) Carbon dioxide 8 Plants make oxygen

2.3
1 a) Ovules (in carpels) b) Pollen (in stamens) 2 In cross-pollination, pollen transferred to flower on different plant 3 By wind, by insects 4 To attract insects 5 Tube grows down to ovary, nucleus passes down tube 6 Fruit 7 Wind, hooks, eaten by animals, flicked from pods 8 Seed starting to grow into plant 9 Protection 10 Plants growing toward light

2.4
1 a) Brain b) Heart and lungs c) Spinal cord 2 Allow bending, absorb jolts 3 Support, allowing movement 4 Calcium; collagen fibres 5 a) Fibres attaching muscles to bones b) Fibres holding joints together 6 Muscles can only contract; antagonistic pairs. 7 Ears send nerve impulses to brain, brain sends nerve impulses to muscles

2.5
1 Broken down into substances which will dissolve 2 Stomach and small intestine 3 Biological catalysts (speed up reactions) 4 Churned, mixed with juice containing enzyme and acid 5 Absorbed into blood 6 Leaves body through anus 7 Carbohydrates, fats, proteins, minerals, vitamins 8 Carbohydrates, fats 9 a) Growth b) Bones and teeth; a) Fish, bread b) Cheese, milk 10 To speed up some chemical reactions 11 Helps food pass along the gut

2.6
1 a) Arteries b) Veins 2 Fine tubes; carry blood near cells 3 To get food and oxygen, and get rid of waste products 4 Plasma 5 White 6 Red; haemoglobin 7 Lungs 8 So blood only flows one way 9 Passes through lungs, heart, other parts of body, heart

2.7
1 a) oxygen b) carbon dioxide (+ water) 2 For blood to absorb/release gases 3 Ribs out, diaphragm down 4 Glycogen, iron, vitamins 5 Removes old red blood cells, produces heat 6 Filtering/cleaning blood 7 Go to bladder 8 They remove unwanted substances from body 9 Lungs

2.8
1 Egg cell; release of egg cell; cycle of egg cell release, uterus lining growth, period 2 28 days 3 Passes out of uterus 4 Must meet sperm 5 In testicles 6 Condom, diaphragm 7 a) Can cause heart, liver, breast disease b) Not very reliable

2.9
1 Chemical instructions needed from both parents for full set 2 Bag of watery liquid 3 Organ which grows into uterus lining where substances can pass between mother's blood and baby's blood 4 & 5 Through placenta and umbilical cord 6 Turns head down; for exit from uterus 7 Substances in mother's blood can get into baby's blood

2.10
1 Contact, animals, droplets in air 2 To avoid contaminating food 3 Some white blood cells digest germs, others make antibodies which kill germs 4 Contain dead or harmless germs which make immune system produce antibodies 5 Exercise, good diet, avoid smoking 6 Stops it working 7 Sexual contact, blood-to-blood contact, infected mother to unborn child

2.11
1 Disease, decomposing food (harmful); making bread, alcohol (useful) 2 Microbe growth stopped by low temperature, lack of liquid 3 If parts undercooked, microbes not killed 4 Keep out microbes in air, low temperature slows microbe growth 5 Making cheese, yoghurt 6 Reaction which changes sugar (glucose) into alcohol (ethanol) and carbon dioxide 7 Gas bubbles from fermentation 8 Biological catalysts (speed up reactions)

2.12
1 Fish, amphibians, reptiles, birds, mammals; backbones 2 All except most mammals 3 Feathers, steady body temperature, lay eggs 4 Mammals; live young which feed on milk 5 A Daisy B Plantain C Yarrow D Rye

2.13
1 Height, weight 2 Tongue-rolling, blood group 3 Chemical instructions for a characteristic; in nucleus of cells 4 One from each parent 5 Same set of genes 6 Features depend on environment 7 Racehorses, wheat 8 Preserve genes

2.14
1 Place where organism lives; group of same organisms; all organisms in one habitat; animal which feeds on other animals 2 Tides cover/uncover beach 3 Temperature change from summer to winter 4 For light and water 5 Has features which help its survival; bear's fur for winter warmth 6 a) Eaten by toads b) Toads have died off, more plants 7 Fewer toads because fewer slugs for food

2.15
1 A Bigger crops, healthier crops B Timber, more crop space C More crop space, easier to harvest D Concrete, steelmaking; A Encourages algae, harms wildlife B destroys habitats, exposes soil C Destroys habitats, encourages pests D Spoils landscape, produces waste 2 Gases from burning fuels 3 Damages stonework, plants, steel 4 Fertilizers, sewage, chemical waste 5 Oil spillages cause pollution

2.16
1 Producers make food, consumers eat it; leaf, snail 2 Materials which rot; leaves, paper 3 Octopus, crab, seal, seagull; populations would fall 4 & 5 See pyramid examples on spread (Q5 biomasses: frog 200 g, worms 10 000 g, leaves 500 000 g)

2.17
1 Photosynthesis 2 Respiration, burning 3 Burning coal makes carbon dioxide which is absorbed by plants, which are eaten by animal 4 For making proteins 5 From nitrates in soil 6 By eating plants 7 By microbes taking nitrogen from air and dead organisms, by the effect of lightning

3.1

1 a) Liquid has no definite shape b) Gas can have any volume **2** a) 1 m^3 of water has a mass of 1000 kg b) 5000 kg **3** Too brittle **4** a) Transparent or translucent b) Hard, strong c) Strong, good conductor (heat) d) Insulator (heat) e) Flexible, insulator (electricity)

3.2

1 Metals, nonmetals **2** Al Fe Ca Na K Mg **3** Hydrogen **4** Compounds are new substances made when elements combine **5** Molecule made from carbon atom and two oxygen atoms **6** Iron reactive, so forms compounds easily, gold unreactive **7** No; reactive, so would have formed compounds

3.3

1 Single substance with nothing mixed in **2** Will dissolve; substance which dissolves; substance it dissolves in; mixture of solvent and solute **3** Mixture of metals **4** Can have best properties of several metals **5** a) Dissolving b) Filtering or distilling c) Chromatography **6** Tea-bag (flavoured water, tea leaves), vacuum-cleaner bag (dust, air)

3.4

1 Dilute acid has more water in **2** Strong acid more corrosive, lower pH **3** Hydrogen **4** Hydrogen; air/hydrogen mixture explodes with pop when lit **5** Salt and water **6** Acidic **7** Slightly alkaline **8** pH7 **9** Indigestion tablet in stomach, toothpaste on teeth

3.5

1 Metals, reactive, one outer shell electron **2** Gases, unreactive, full outer shells **3** a) 2 b) 6 **4** Kr is unreactive gas, 36 electrons in full shells; Cs is reactive metal, 55 electrons, one in outer shell; Co is magnetic metal, 27 electrons **5** Neon has full outer shell, sodium has one outer shell electron

3.6

1 a) Particles in liquid can change positions b) Particles in gas not held together, can move about freely **2** Move faster **3** a) 0 ^oC b) 100 ^oC **4** Particles wander, jostled by other particles; diffusion **5** Particles vibrate more, push each other apart **6** To allow for contraction ('shrinking') when temperature falls

3.7

1 a) 273 K b) 373 K c) 300 K d) 200 K **2** a) P proportional to T b) V proportional to T c) P increases if V decreases d) P proportional to $1/V$ **3** a) Particles packed into smaller space, so more strike each mm^2 of balloon b) Temperature rises, particles hit sides of canister faster **4** 12 m^3

3.8

1 a) Proton b) Electron c) Neutron **2** 5 **3** Charged atoms **4** Covalent bonds (shared electrons) **5** Bonds more easily broken **6** Ions separate and spread between water molecules

3.9

1 a) Total of protons + neutrons b) Same number of protons (and electrons) c) Different numbers of neutrons **2** Has atoms with unstable nuclei **3** Removes electrons from atoms **4** Can kill or damage cells **5** Alpha, beta, gamma **6** Alpha **7** Gamma **8** Alpha **9** Small amount of radiation always present from natural sources

3.10

1 Reversible, no new substance formed **2** a) Magnesium oxide b) Exothermic; gives out heat **3** Powdered magnesium; bigger surface area for reaction **4** a) Decomposition b) Substance which speeds up reaction without being used up

c) glucose $\xrightarrow{\text{yeast}}$ ethanol + carbon dioxide

3.11

1 Heat, air (oxygen), fuel **2** An oxide **3** Carbon dioxide and water **4** a) Turns lime water milky b) Makes smouldering splint burst into flames **5** Air (oxygen) and water **6** Makes fats rancid; refrigerating, keeping out oxygen

3.12

1 To produce carbon monoxide for reaction which releases iron from ore **2** Electrolysis **3** Copper ions (+) attracted to cathode (–) **4** Impurities burnt off, then carbon added **5** a) Aluminium b) Gold; very unreactive c) Aluminium; most readily forms compounds, so most difficult to remove from compounds

3.13

1 a) Treating icy roads, flavouring food, preserving food b) Sodium hydroxide, sodium, chlorine **2** a) Water b) Chlorine c) Purifying water, making PVC, bleach, pesticides, solvents **3** Chippings, making cement

3.14

1 Compounds of hydrogen and carbon **2** Petrol, diesel oil, kerosene **3** Breaking long molecules into shorter molecules; to match supply of different oil fractions to demand **4** Nitrogen; preserving food, quickfreezing food **5** Passing methane and steam over catalysts, electrolysing sodium chloride solution, electrolysing acidified water **6** Hydrogen, helium; helium; does not burn **7** Distillation (different substances boiled off at different temperatures)

3.15

1 Millions of tiny water droplets; water vapour condenses when temperature falls **2** Water vapour in air condenses and freezes; water expands when it freezes **3** Pressure readings in mb getting less **4** Warm, damp air being pushed up and cooled **5** They pass over sea **6** Make moving air rise and cool **7** Dry; winds blow from dry land

3.16

1 Water goes from drains to sea, evaporates to form clouds, rain falls over reservoir **2** Building reservoirs changes landscape, destroys habitats, taking water from ground can dry it out **3** Wearing away of surfaces **4** Particles transported, deposited as sediments, crushed to form new rock **5** Rock underneath; rock gets broken up by frost, rain, expansion due to Sun's heat

3.17

1 Molten rock from under Earth's surface **2** Magma cools, solidifies **3** Quick cooling gives smaller crystals **4** Layers of sediment crushed, then set hard **5** a) Can form from sediments containing remains of dead organisms b) Formed from very hot, molten material **6** Metamorphic; limestone, changed by heat **7** No advantages; disadvantages a) Not easy to split into layers b) Not so hard, attacked by acid rain

4.1

1 Metals, carbon **2** negative (–) **3** Like charges repel **4** a) Positive (+) b) Negative (–) **5** Break in conducting path, so circuit not complete

4.2

1 Ammeter; 2.0 **2** Voltmeter **3** a) Brighter b) Higher c) Higher (approx double) **4** a) Reduced to previous brightness b) Reduced to previous value (2.0) **5** Brightness not reduced; one bulb keeps working if other bulb removed

4.3

1 Lower resistance; resistance too high, heat given off, current reduced **2** Heating elements; because high resistance gives heating effect **3** Brighter; less resistance, so higher current **4** 2 kW h; 20p **5** a) 80p b) 10p **6** 160p

4.4
1 AND gate **2** Both OFF **3** Output is always opposite of input **4** a) AND b) OR gate

4.5
1 With a compass **2** More turns on coil, higher current **3** Wrap coil round nail, connect coil to battery **4** Small current switches on electromagnet in relay, relay switches on motor circuit **5** Electromagnet gets stronger as current rises, minimum force needed to release catch **6** Cone must vibrate to give out sound, so magnetic force must be backwards, forwards .. and so on

4.6
1 a) Connecting outside circuit to coil b) Reversing current through coil every half turn **2** Stronger magnet, more turns on coil, higher current **3** AC keeps changing direction; a) DC b) AC c) AC **4** a) By turning coil in magnetic field b) To connect coil to outside circuit **5** Changing voltage; AC

4.7
1 a) Moving car b) Battery c) Stretched spring **2** 10 000 J **3** Chemical; changed to heat + kinetic energy **4** Kinetic → heat **5** Chemical → kinetic → potential → kinetic → heat **6** Energy can change forms, but total amount stays the same

4.8
1 Conduction and convection need particles to carry energy, space empty; radiation **2** Hot air rises, cooler air replaces it and is heated **3** a) Air very poor conductor b) To reflect Sun's radiation c) Poor radiators of heat **4** a) Part-vacuum b) Stopper c) Shiny surfaces; reduces heat flow in either direction

4.9 and 4.10
1 Cannot be replaced; coal, oil **2** Global warming (carbon dioxide), acid rain (sulphur dioxide) **3** Hydroelectric scheme, aerogenerators **4** Ancient sea plants absorbed Sun's energy, ancient sea creatures fed on plants, remains of plants and creatures trapped and crushed by sediment to form oil, petrol extracted from oil **5** 25% of fuel's energy changed into kinetic energy, rest wasted as heat **6** Less fuel burnt, so supplies last longer and less pollution

4.11
1 500 N **2** Forces are weight (500 N downwards), air resistance (500 N upwards); resultant 0 **3** a) With flat shoes, force spread over larger area so pressure less b) Pressure from water produces upward force which balances weight **4** 200 Pa

4.12
1 To give turning effect which matches turning effect of load, so that centre of mass of crane and load is over base **2** When load is changed, turning effect of counterbalance must be changed **3** 200 N m **4** 200 N m **5** 0.5 m **6** 200 N (counterbalance is then at max distance) **7** Wider base, heavier weight low down on base

4.13
1 10 m/s **2** Head-down position, shaped helmet, smooth & tight-fitting outfit, streamlined bike (e.g no spokes) **3** a) Brakes, tyres, steering wheel b) Wheel bearings, moving parts of engine and gearbox, car body moving through air **4** a) 15 m b) 18 m; at higher speed, car travels further in same time **5** a) 50 m b) 99 m

4.14
1 Pliers, nutcrackers, can opener **2** Energy output would be greater than energy input, which breaks law of conservation of energy **3** 100 J **4** 10 W **5** 100 W

4.15
1 Solid, liquid, or gas needed to carry vibrations **2** Microphone + CRO, seeing wave trace on screen **3** Sound much slower than light **4** 660 m **5** a) $1/3$ s b) $2/3$ s after he shouts **6** Using echo to measure depth of water; sound reflected from sea-bed, echo time measured, longer time means greater depth of water **7** Sound keeps reflecting from walls; putting sound-absorbing materials (curtains, carpet) in room

4.16
1 a) Vibrates when sound waves strike it b) Transmit vibrations to cochlea c) Sensor cells respond to vibrations and send nerve impulses to brain **2** Very high amplitude sound waves can damage ear drum, cochlea, or auditory nerve **3** 200 sound waves every second **4** a) Louder b) Higher pitch **5** Safer (do not damage/destroy body cells); checking unborn baby in womb

4.17
1 Reflects daylight or other lighting **2** Wall scatters light, mirror reflects light in regular way **3** For straight-ahead view and image which is right way round **4** Bending of light when it enters/leaves transparent material; light entering glass block **5** Light waves on one side of beam reach glass first and slow before those on other side, so beam bends; both sides of beam reach glass at same time and slow together **6** Thin, flexible, rod of glass/plastic which transmits light; light zig-zags along fibre as it reflects from side to side

4.18
1 a) Smaller, upright b) Larger, upright **2** Camera (forms image on film, eye (forms image on retina), projector (forms image on screen) **3** Convex lens system, aperture control, upside-down image on retina/film **4** For distant object, short-sighted eye focuses light in front of retina, not on it; concave; to spread rays before they enter eye

4.19
1 Violet; shorter wavelength, slowed more by glass **2** radio, micro, infrared, light, ultraviolet, X-rays, gamma **3** a) Light b) radio, micro, light (+ infrared in remote controllers) c) infrared, micro d) X-rays, gamma e) X-rays, gamma

4.20
1 a) 27 days b) just over 365 days **2** Earth's axis tilted so that north angled towards Sun in June, away from Sun in December **3** Time for Moon's orbit same as time for rotation **4** Reflects Sun's light **5** Crescent is sunlit part, rest is in shadow **6** Less **7** Earth turning at same rate as satellite orbiting

4.21
1 Jupiter **2** Mercury, Venus, Mars, Pluto **3** Mars, Jupiter, Saturn, Uranus, Neptune, Pluto; further from Sun, so receive less heat **4** Jupiter, Saturn, Uranus, Neptune **5** Reflect Sun's light **6** Greater distance, longer orbit time **7** Venus hotter than Mercury, yet further from Sun **8** a) Star system with billions of stars b) Distance travelled by light in one year **9** Andromeda; 2 million years; take too long as nothing can travel faster than light

Index

Periodic table

Group

I	II											III	IV	V	VI	VII	O

Period																		
1							H hydrogen 1											He helium 2
2	Li lithium 3	Be beryllium 4											B boron 5	C carbon 6	N nitrogen 7	O oxygen 8	F fluorine 9	Ne neon 10
3	Na sodium 11	Mg magnesium 12											Al aluminium 13	Si silicon 14	P phosphorus 15	S sulphur 16	Cl chlorine 17	Ar argon 18
4	K potassium 19	Ca calcium 20	Sc scandium 21	Ti titanium 22	V vanadium 23	Cr chromium 24	Mn manganese 25	Fe iron 26	Co cobalt 27	Ni nickel 28	Cu copper 29	Zn zinc 30	Ga gallium 31	Ge germanium 32	As arsenic 33	Se selenium 34	Br bromine 35	Kr krypton 36
5	Rb rubidium 37	Sr strontium 38	Y yttrium 39	Zr zirconium 40	Nb niobium 41	Mo molybdenum 42	Tc technetium 43	Ru ruthenium 44	Rh rhodium 45	Pd palladium 46	Ag silver 47	Cd cadmium 48	In indium 49	Sn tin 50	Sb antimony 51	Te tellurium 52	I iodine 53	Xe xenon 54
6	Cs caesium 55	Ba barium 56	La lanthanum 57	Hf hafnium 72	Ta tantalum 73	W tungsten 74	Re rhenium 75	Os osmium 76	Ir iridium 77	Pt platinum 78	Au gold 79	Hg mercury 80	Tl thallium 81	Pb lead 82	Bi bismuth 83	Po polonium 84	At astatine 85	Rn radon 86
7	Fr francium 87	Ra radium 88	Ac actinium 89															

Ce cerium 58	Pr praseodymium 59	Nd neodymium 60	Pm promethium 61	Sm samarium 62	Eu europium 63	Gd gadolinium 64	Tb terbium 65	Dy dysprosium 66	Ho holmium 67	Er erbium 68	Tm thulium 69	Yb ytterbium 70	Lu lutetium 71
Th thorium 90	Pa protactinium 91	U uranium 92	Np neptunium 93	Pu plutonium 94	Am americium 95	Cm curium 96	Bk berkelium 97	Cf californium 98	Es einsteinium 99	Fm fermium 100	Md mendelevium 101	No nobelium 102	Lr lawrencium 103